D0886892

Ernie Davis:
The Elmira Express

The Story of a
Heisman Trophy Winner

By Robert C. Gallagher
With a Remembrance by Floyd Little

1983

Bartleby Press

Silver Spring, Maryland

Excerpts in this edition appear with the permission of:

Boy's Life: A publication of Boy Scouts of America
The Cleveland Press
Chicago Tribune
Elmira *Star-Gazette*
Los Angeles Herald Examiner
Philadelphia Bulletin
The San Francisco Examiner
Syracuse Herald - American
Sport Magazine
© 1960, 1961 by *Playboy* Magazine
© *The Washington Post*
Life Magazine, Time, Inc. Reprinted with permission
New York Herald Tribune © IHT Corporation Reprinted with Permission
© 1963/80 by The New York Times Company. Reprinted with Permission.
Excerpts from *Off My Chest* by Jim Brown and Myron Cope © 1964, Jim Brown and Myron Cope. Reprinted by Permission of Doubleday & Co., Inc.
Excerpts from *PB: The Paul Brown Story* by Paul Brown with Jack Clary are reprinted with the permission of Atheneum Publishers. © 1979 by Paul Brown and Jack Clary
Reprinted from *The Saturday Evening Post* © 1963 by Curtis Publishing Company.

Library of Congress Catalog Card Number 83 - 71997
ISBN 0-910155-03-8

Published and distributed by:

Bartleby Press
11141 Georgia Avenue
Suite A-6
Silver Spring, Maryland 20902

Printed in the United States of America

Contents

To my family, Mom, Dad, Matthew, and Paula,
for their vital contributions

A Remembrance

In my 21 years of playing football I received over 150 trophies and plaques but I keep only one in my office, The Ernie Davis Memorial Award from the Coaches All-America game. The plaque has a picture of Ernie and is given to the player who best exemplifies his qualities.

To this day I can vividly recall how impressed I was by Ernie. We first met when he visited my home in New Haven, Connecticut, with coach Ben Schwartzwalder, to recruit me for Syracuse University. I remember his size and how well-dressed he was. We went to dinner and Ernie took me aside. He briefly mentioned football and then emphasized the importance of an education. He said I would receive an academic scholarship which would guarantee my education as long as I maintained the academic standards. "I haven't done badly," he said, "for a guy who didn't have a dime." That conversation is how I remember him.

My entire family was impressed by him. My mother said, "If that school graduates a person like Ernie, you should consider going there." My three sisters fell in love with him. In a letter he wrote of how much he enjoyed meeting my family and mentioned each of my sisters by name.

At that time, I was also being heavily recruited by the University of Notre Dame. In fact I had committed to the

Fighting Irish. I have a newspaper article with the head-line, "Little Goes to Notre Dame." I was reluctant to admit it to Ernie, however, and led him to believe I would go to Syracuse. When Ernie died I felt obligated to fulfill my promise to him. I called coach Schwartzwalder and told him I'd be coming to Syracuse. It was one of the better decisions I ever made.

So many people loved Ernie at Syracuse because he spread so much love. He didn't have to be loud or the center of attention. You just knew he was there.

As a collegian I felt a tremendous responsibility to up-hold the tradition Jim Brown and Ernie established. It was a great honor to be mentioned in the same breath with them. Everytime I put on the jersey number 44, they both wore, I thought about them. They were the best.

Courage to me was Ernie's outstanding quality. To excel as an athlete you have to play with pain. There is a dif-ference between pain and injury. An athlete has to deal with pain. "Put a band aid on it and play," is the credo. The only way they can get you off the field is by hiding your uniform or by dragging you off kicking and screaming. Ernie exemplified that determination throughout his life particularly while fighting against leukemia. He never quit.

Since Ernie's death I have been involved in many cere-monies honoring him. The first intercollegiate football game I ever saw, Ernie's mother presented his Heisman Trophy to the University. When he was inducted into the College Football Hall of Fame, during a game at Meadow-lands Stadium, Jim Brown and I escorted his mother on to the field. Whenever I've seen her throughout the years, I've made a conscious effort to represent Ernie and try to emulate his qualities.

Today there is a need for heroes. The pressures and challenges of life may seem overwhelming, particularly to youngsters. Heroes like Ernie Davis, provide inspiration, incentive, and direction. I immensely enjoyed reading his inspirational story and I'm sure you will too.

Floyd Little

Background

A young man's first hero often remains more sharply etched in his memory than his first love. Mine was Ernest R. Davis, who in 1961 became the first black football player to win the Heisman Trophy. He died of leukemia 18 months later without fulfilling his dream of playing professional football. Despite the tragedy of a life cut short, his story is more than a cheers-to-tears heartbreaker. Although fans recall an athlete and his achievements, friends remember a man and his character.

I never met Ernie personally, yet throughout my life by chance, coincidence or the reminiscence of a mutual acquaintance, I would often recall his memory. I became a fan of his when I was ten years old playing football in the backyards, fields, and streets of my neighborhood, and like many other boys my age, I dreamed of being an All-American, a Heisman Trophy winner, and even an All-Pro.

I lived in the Northern Virginia suburbs of Washington, D.C. The big college star of that time was, Joe Bellino, All-American halfback and Heisman Trophy winner from the United States Naval Academy only 40 miles away in Annapolis, Maryland. We neighborhood boys used to vie for the honor of playing Joe Bellino in our pickup football games. I don't remember why we wanted to be college players rather than pros. Possibly because the pros hadn't yet earned the popularity they now enjoy or because the college players were closer to our age.

One day when another boy "called" Joe Bellino first, I said, "Okay, I'm going to be Ernie Davis of Syracuse." A playmate shouted, "You can't be Ernie Davis, he's a nigger." Then to everybody else, "He wants to be a nigger." I answered, "He's an All-American," which to me was a comeback of unassailable logic. I can't honestly say I was morally indignant. I was embarrassed. I had never experienced bigotry and didn't understand it. I wonder why a person could dislike someone because of their color. Stubbornly, I stuck with my choice.

Months later I discovered why the boy acted the way he did. In December 1961 we interrupted our football game in that same kid's yard to watch the Syracuse-Miami Liberty Bowl game. Ernie and the Syracuse team played poorly in the first half. As we went out to throw the ball around during halftime, my playmate, remembering my earlier statement said, "I told you Ernie Davis wasn't any good. He's a nigger." My embarrassment increased when his father said, "None of those niggers are any good." While we were outside I silently prayed, with the fervor only a youngster praying for a hero can muster, that Ernie play well in the second half. With trepidation I went in to watch the rest of the game.

As if in answer to my prayers, Ernie played magnificently in the second half and rallied Syracuse to victory. At game's end in righteous indignation I asked, "What do you think of Ernie Davis now?" My friend's father answered, "He's still a nigger." I didn't respond, but I secretly gloated at the man's discomfort.

At that time Washington sports fans were eagerly anticipating watching Ernie play with the hometown Redskins, which had ostensibly made him the number one selection in the 1962 National Football League draft. I was disappointed when it was later announced that Ernie, in fact, had been traded by Washington to the Cleveland Browns prior to the draft.

After weighing offers from both the Browns and the Buffalo Bills of the rival American Football League, Ernie signed a then NFL record-setting rookie contract with Cleveland. However, his professional career ended before it began at the College All-Stars training camp.

I remember my disappoinment when it was reported Ernie would not play in the annual exhibition game due to illness. Later, the newspapers described his condition as a "blood disorder," which would prevent Ernie's playing during the 1962 football season. Although I'm sure that privately he was devastated by the news, publicly Ernie never changed. For months he had been signing autographs, "Ernie Davis, Cleveland Browns, 1962." Despite the setback, he never gave up hope that he would overcome his illness. Eight weeks later, there was finally some good news. Ernie Davis had leukemia, but it was in total remission, and as long as the remission lasted, the doctors said Ernie could play football. According to the newspapers, the Brown's management was divided over whether he should play. Ultimately Coach Paul Brown chose not to activate him.

During the winter of 1963, Ernie's leukemia returned and within four months he died. One can imagine the crushing disappointment of the young athlete when he learned that his battle with the disease had not been won. By all accounts his fears and disappointments remained a private agony. To the outside world he turned his usual confident smiling face, betraying not a hint of concern about his health or his prospects as an athlete. John Brown, Ernie's teammate at Syracuse University and roommate in Cleveland, scoffed when asked what it was like to watch a young man die. "I don't know," he said, "I watched a young man live."

Ernest R. Davis, 23, died of leukemia on May 18, 1963. The courage and dignity Ernie showed in facing death stirred a city and a country. In one day over 10,000 people filed past Ernie's coffin, as he lay in state in his hometown of Elmira, New York. Thousands attended the funeral which was sadly one of the biggest events in Elmira history. Certainly anyone who was there will never forget it.

President John F. Kennedy sent Ernie's mother a telegram of condolence, which read, "I would like to express my sympathy to you on the occasion of the death of your son. I had the privilege of meeting Ernie after he won the Heisman Trophy. He was an outstanding young man of great character who consistently served as an inspiration to the other people of the country."

I never heard much about Ernie Davis after his death until I enrolled at Syracuse University four years later. There I met people who had known him. I was intrigued listening to their anecdotes about what a great person he was. They rarely talked about him as an athlete. At a freshman orientation lecture, Dr. Michael O. Sawyer, now a university vice chancellor, described his last encounter with Ernie Davis. Two weeks before his death, Ernie visited the campus and called Sawyer to arrange a visit. The professor, aware of the gravity of Ernie's condition, was concerned about how to talk to a young man of such extraordinary ability and potential who had only a short time to live. Sawyer's concerns proved unwarranted because Ernie controlled the conversation by asking about Sawyer, his plans, and mutual acquaintances. He didn't allow the professor to feel uncomfortable.

Eighteen years later, Sawyer was still impressed by the "stylish performance." He said, "In those circumstances, most peoples' concerns would have been totally centered on their own illness or their own problems, but he was so sensitive to other people. He was always interested in others and their well being. I was always impressed by him."

Since graduating from Syracuse University, I continued to have unexpected reminders of Ernie Davis. In the fall of 1979, a former classmate invited me to the Syracuse-Penn State football game at the Meadowlands Stadium in East Rutherford, New Jersey. We didn't know that during halftime ceremonies, Ernie Davis would be inducted into the

College Football Hall of Fame. The emotional induction and the subsequent newspaper stories gave me a few more memories. Still more unexpected was a chance encounter with a co-worker on that Monday following the induction ceremony. Hearing me speak about Syracuse, the lady volunteered that she was from Elmira, New York. Since that was Ernie's hometown, I idly asked if she knew who "The Elmira Express" was. She responded, "You mean Ernie?" Incredulously I asked, "Did you know him?" She answered, "Of course, everybody in Elmira knew Ernie. He was a terrific guy."

I decided to find out if it was true. To satisfy my curiosity, I began reading the old newspaper and magazine stories about him in the local library. It quickly became apparent that Ernie Davis was a young man of extraordinary character and courage as well as athletic skill. I felt his story deserved a wider audience.

I began contacting those who knew him, some well and others casually. They had similar impressions and used the same descriptive words; "concerned for others," "self-aware," "modest," "leader," and "great sense of humor." Also, they all willingly took time from their busy schedules to discuss their feelings for Ernie. They often said, "I'm really busy, but I'll do it for Ernie."

You might expect such reactions from friends, but hardly from those in athletics where fame is ephemeral and an athlete's only as good as his last game. Ernie's last game was over 20 years ago. Although those close to him obviously remember his athletic skill, it is as a person that he is most vividly remembered.

His high school football coach, Marty Harrigan, now the school's principal, states, "Ernie Davis was more than a jock. He was something really special. He loved his fellow man and wanted to do things for him. Do them quietly and do them by example." Tony DeFilippo, lawyer and advisor said, "It was always what could he do for the other guy. Everyone who knew the truth about him would say the same thing."

Mention Syracuse University and sports fans invariably recall such football stars as Jim Brown, John Mackey, Jim Nance, Floyd Little, and Larry Csonka. I always added "Ernie Davis", and they would nod and reply, "Too bad he died. He would have been great." That observation missed the point. Obviously his untimely death was tragic, but, the "ifs" of Ernie's life were not as important as the "whats" and "hows".

Through his concern for others and his self-confidence, particularly as he faced death, Ernie Davis was a greater hero than he ever would have been as a professional football superstar. In his final months Ernie experienced the emotional high points and low points of his life. The personal courage and dignity he demonstrated were remarkable. As in all endeavors, Ernie did his best to overcome leukemia. When he couldn't, he didn't curse the fates. He was thankful for what he had attained.

Roommate John Brown, who played ten years in the NFL, remembered one of the few times he ever saw Ernie angry. "He had taken a date to the movies and while they were standing outside, a man asked, 'Are you Ernie Davis?' Not wanting to invite attention he said, 'No.' The stranger stated, 'You're lucky. Ernie Davis has leukemia. He's only got six months to live.' " Shocked by the man's callousness, Ernie confronted him angrily and said, "I am Ernie Davis and I'm going to live." When he came home to the apartment, he told John Brown what happened. "Ernie couldn't get over the guy saying something like that to a stranger," recalled Brown. "He said, I didn't want to embarrass him, but it might keep him from being cruel to someone else."

If willpower alone could cure cancer, Ernie would have been cured instantly. He had overcome obstacles before and he firmly believed he could in this case. When it became obvious he would not, Ernie wrote an article for *The Saturday Evening Post* magazine titled "I'm Not Unlucky". It was a striking testament to his courage. Without the least trace of self-pity, Ernie steadfastly maintained that he was a fortunate man and that his accomplishments were their own reward.

Tony DeFilippo, Ernie's lawyer who negotiated his record professional football contract, was visiting him in Cleveland when the leukemia returned. They were riding in a taxi and a book fell from Ernie's coat pocket. The title was *Burial Masses*. Despite his fierce determination to live and his unfailing confident public demeanor, Ernie obviously had a clear perception of the gravity of his condition and was determined to face it. He did so with tremendous personal courage and his characteristic concern for others rather than himself.

A few weeks prior to his death Ernie visited friends at Syracuse and Elmira. The day he checked into the hospital for the final time, he visited the Cleveland Browns' offices. He never said good-bye, but when he died soon afterward, everyone realized that had probably been his intention.

Elmira lawyer Jack Moore, a high school basketball teammate recalled the last time he saw Ernie. Despite his condition, Ernie maintained a buoyant attitude and sought to reassure others. They went to a local restaurant and as always happened wherever Ernie went in Elmira, a crowd gathered around the table. The young waitress, on recognizing Ernie, began to cry because she had read and heard he was dying of leukemia. Ernie patted her on the hand and smiled, I know they have me dead and buried, but don't worry, I've got this thing licked. I feel great. I'm looking forward to playing football this season.' The waitress began beaming and we all felt better. He convinced us. When he died a few weeks later, it was obvious he had been well aware of his condition. It was important to him to make the waitress and the rest of us feel better no matter how he felt."

Ernie's concern for others was a natural outgrowth of his own self-confidence. He knew where he was and where he was going. Although he achieved tremendous athletic success, he never allowed his fame to dominate his life. Former high school and college teammate Bill Fitzgerald remembered, "Ernie had at an early age what others don't get until their 70's—wisdom and understanding. People came to him because he was strong and never turned anybody off."

Conversations about his athletic accomplishments were always initiated by others. Ernie understood the fans' interest and was patient in responding to their inquiries. Unlike today's braggadoccio style athletes, he never felt compelled to talk about himself. Once at a party in Cleveland, someone introduced him to a young woman as "Ernie Davis, the Heisman Trophy winner." She responded, "So?" Instead of being offended, Ernie laughed in agreement. He spent the remainder of the evening talking and dancing with her.

Ernie gave evidence of his inner strength and concern for others even in his youth. No one interviewed could give an explanation of why Ernie had these characteristics. They simply said, "That was just Ernie." Whatever the reason, the impression was lasting. John Brown named a son after him, and Ernie's mother was the child's godmother. He said, "I hope both my boys grow up to be like Ernie." Syracuse University football coach Ben Schwartzwalder, who coached hundreds of young men during his 25 year career, said of him, "I never met another human being as good as Ernie."

Part of growing up is realizing that childhood heroes whoever they might be—older relatives, public figures, athletic stars—are still human beings. Save for an extraordinary ability or quality they possess, they are subject to the same problems, fears, failures, and worries that others have.

Ernie Davis was not superhuman. All those interviewed were careful not to portray him in exaggerated terms, but they clearly saw something in him that they recognized as out of the ordinary. The fact that his peers recognized these qualities and struggled to find words to describe them was particularly impressive. They dwelt on his courage, his personal warmth, and most of all his feeling for others. They acknowledged his human failings, and they also admired his humane character.

These characteristics were conveyed in many different ways by relatives and friends. In addition to information, they provided an almost tangible sense of the psychological and emotional environment that shaped his life. Although a disparate group, they were united in their admiration for Ernie Davis. It was easy to get to know him through them.

One of the first people interviewed was Ernie's mother, Marie Fleming. She seemed to be wary at first and before consenting to an interview asked a number of questions about my motives. We met in her comfortable home in Elmira. Ernie was meticulous in appearance and after visiting his mother's home, it was obvious that she was the influence.

Trophies, plaques, and photographs of Ernie were clearly visible. Mrs. Fleming was tall and younger looking than expected. Unaccustomed to being interviewed, her initial answers were short, but as the interview progressed, she relaxed and became more expansive in her responses. At the end she recommended interviewing her brother, Chuck Davis, and Ernie's friend, John Brown, both of whom were invaluable.

Chuck Davis proved to be an important source of information about Ernie's childhood. Because of Ernie's and Mrs. Fleming's height and the fact that Chuck had been a college basketball player, a tall man was expected. But he is short and powerfully built. He still looked like he could play a good game.

The interview took place at his office in lower Manhattan where he is a liaison for special services for children in direct child care. We met in a conference room and the extension cord for the tape recorder did not reach the outlet. Chuck and some co-workers searched until they found a cord long enough. Rather than being nervous or wary, Chuck was completely relaxed and made the interview seem like old friends talking. He has a great sense of humor and an engaging laugh. His whole body would move in his chair as he stomped his foot or slapped his hand on the table. Normally a single two hour cassette is sufficient for an interview, but we went through two cassettes and talked for an additional couple of hours.

I had already missed my scheduled return flight by the time we left his office. Chuck accompanied me to the lobby where we continued to talk, while office workers walked between us on their way home. We finally broke up when the head of the crew buffing the lobby floor said, "Let's go fellas. I've been working around you for over an hour." Chuck went on to an NAACP dinner. I scrambled to make another flight home.

John Brown, another important source of information, is a big bear of a man. You would immediately assume he was a former football player. When he walks upstairs you know it. Non-football players take a step at a time putting one foot on each stair. Former football players like Brown who have had knee operations, step with their good leg and bring the sore leg up to the same stair each time.

As many others would, John gave long answers to the questions. They were monologues. One recollection would quickly lead to another. He didn't seem to hold anything back. The affection John had for Ernie was obvious, and there was no inhibition about expressing it to a stranger. This was particularly striking due to the "tough guy" image of football players. John's recollections were also impressive because they were of Ernie as a man. His only short answers were to questions about athletics.

Lawyer Tony DeFilippo was interviewed in his office in Elmira. Now in his seventies, he is a grandfatherly figure. He makes you feel he has taken you into his confidence. In a conspiratorial tone he'd say, "turn that [tape recorder] off. Fix that one up a little bit." It was obvious that if the wheeler dealers in professional football dismissed him as a small-town lawyer, they were mistaken. Ernie's record contract attests to that.

Tony could not recall the exact name of the church where Ernie's funeral service was held. He asked his secretary, who thought it was a Baptist church. She came in with the Yellow Pages and they found what they thought was the church. Tony grabbed the phone and called to confirm it. He made recommendations of others to contact and said, "If you have any trouble, give me a call." I never had to take him up on the offer.

Last to be interviewed was John Mackey, Ernie's roommate for three years at Syracuse, before becoming a professional football star as a tight end for the Baltimore Colts. His wife, Sylvia Mackey, who attended Syracuse with them, also participated. We met in their large Spanish style home in California. As a former President of the National Football League Players Association, who led the first pro football strike, Mackey has a formidable reputation. It's unwarranted. John Mackey is an interesting and humorous man. He laughs easily and he doesn't just tell a story, he performs it.

Mackey characterized the difference between college football players of his era and today's. He also gave insights into Ernie as an athlete. There's a large window in Mackey's living room with a view of the snow-capped San Gabriel Mountains. Pointing at the window he stated, "When Ernie and I played, if the coach told you to run through that window, you'd run through that window. Ernie would run through that window and probably have perfect form. Today guys would ask, what's running through that window got to do with playing football?"

Sylvia Mackey provided a feminine non-athletic perspective on Ernie's college life. After pondering for a time she said, "I'm trying to recall some story about Ernie, but I can't. Ernie was the nicest of all the athletes. He carried himself well. He was most respectful of the girls." Eventually she remembered an incident. "Ernie had this nice orange sweater," she said. "One day I saw him wearing it while walking across campus, and I told him how much I liked it. He asked if I wanted it? I thought he was kidding, so I said, 'yes.' He took it off on the spot and gave it to me. I wore it to all the games for good luck. I still have it in a trunk. I should get it out. It was a pretty sweater."

Ernie's impact extended beyond family and friends.

While writing this·book I accidentally met people who knew Ernie casually but retain vivid memories of him. One person who was from Elmira spoke warmly of his childhood days and of being coached by Ernie Davis. Another was a classmate of Ernie's at Syracuse University. He recalled the influence Ernie had on the campus. A woman who had been a secretary for the Cleveland Browns, when Ernie signed with them, recalled his strong personal relationship with the team's president Art Modell.

In his sophomore year Ernie's performance against the University of Pittsburgh inspired the nickname, "The Elmira Express". Al Mallette, sports editor of the Elmira *Star-Gazette*, was sitting in the pressbox that day. After Ernie had run "the scissors play" for a touchdown, he turned to a colleague from Pittsburgh and said, "The Elmira Express roared today". The metaphor also describes his life. He came through quickly, but the stops were memorable.

Uniontown

On the surface, Ernie's childhood seemed less than idyllic, but on closer examination it appears to have been filled with positive experiences. Shortly after his birth on December 14, 1939, in New Salem, Pennsylvania, his parents separated. Soon thereafter Ernie's father, whom he never knew, was killed in an accident. At 14 months, Ernie's mother brought him to live with her parents Willie and Elizabeth Davis, who had 12 children of their own. The family soon moved to Uniontown, 52 miles south of Pittsburgh, where Ernie lived until the age of 12.

The Davis family lived in an eight-room house across the street from the apartment housing project in Uniontown. His grandparents, whom Ernie called "Mom" and "Dad", instilled traditional values—loyalty, discipline, religion, and the importance of an education. "Mom" was the homemaker and primary disciplinarian. When she called one of the children—especially by his full name—the kids knew they'd better come running. "Dad", a coal miner, worked six days a week in the mines for 42 years. He survived three cave-ins, including being buried underground four days. He died in his early seventies of black lung disease. While there were insecurities in Ernie's early life, his grandparents' family provided a sense of identity and belonging. His grandfather was a strong father figure, and his two uncles, close in age to him, were like older brothers. His aunts were like sisters. With so many vying for parental attention, Ernie ran little risk of becoming a spoiled child. Indeed, his strong feeling of concern for others, which many of his contemporaries mentioned as one of his salient traits, was no doubt nurtured in the caring atmosphere of his adopted family.

Admittedly unfamiliar with Ernie's childhood in Uniontown, sportswriter Al Mallette of Elmira said, "Apparently, he had terrific grandparents. They taught him to be humble, generous, appreciative and religious. He learned to give love. He grew from a great kid to a great man."

Much of the information about Ernie's childhood comes from an uncle two years his elder, a wiry, gregarious, open hearted man named Chuck Davis. Many of Chuck's recollections concerned the commonplace experiences of childhood, but Chuck relayed them with earnestness and enthusiasm. It was palpably evident that he hoped that by evoking his personal recollections of Ernie's childhood he might help reveal the private side of his nephew/brother. In fact, his stories did convey a sense of the texture of Ernie's early life.

Ernie's early years are by all measures the most difficult period of his life to reconstruct. His childhood was not extraordinary, quite the contrary, and that's the problem. There was little about the child or his family circumstances to cause contemporaries to anticipate his future fame, and hence take special notice of his youthful activities that would interest a future biographer. It is thus not surprising that family members and friends were often at a loss to supply significant detail when asked to recall their memories of Ernie's childhood. Nevertheless, what came through strong and clear was the image of a good, dutiful, but fun-loving boy, whom everybody seemed to love. If he was not quite a model of all the virtues, he was, it seemed, a fair reflection of the sturdy, tough-spirited, God-fearing people from whom he came.

Religion was an important element in Ernie's childhood and later life. His faith was apparently a fixed star in his universe, a set of beliefs and a way of living that he accepted easily and without question. He went to Baptist church services regularly, and he frequently referred to God in his public speeches. Chuck Davis recalled that once when Ernie asked him to attend church he declined, saying he'd think about God at home. Ernie replied, " 'Radios, newspapers and phones cause too many distractions at home. That's why there are churches so you can concentrate on God.' "

John Mackey recalled that, while they were roommates at Syracuse, Ernie got down on his knees every night and prayed. Mackey, whose father was a minister, said that Ernie regularly suggested going to church on Sundays. "If I'd had a rough Saturday night, I'd say, 'If there's a God he can hear us from here,' and then I'd roll over. Ernie would go to church."

Ernie's belief in the presence of God in his life is illustrated by another Mackey story. "We were going to the movies one day," he recalled "when admissions were 50 cents and he had a dollar to treat us. A lady approached us begging. Without a moment's hesitation, Ernie gave her the dollar. I said, 'Are you crazy? She's just going to buy booze with that.' 'It doesn't matter,' he said, 'God knew my intention when I gave it to her.' "

Jack Moore, who had seen Ernie just a few weeks before his death, felt that he was at peace with himself. "He never talked much about religion," Moore said. "He must have had some kind of overriding belief in God because I don't think he could have handled his dying the way he did without that." He had a true sense of who he was and where he was.

Another important factor in Ernie's life was that he stuttered as a child. At that time, a speech handicap was a significant impediment because elementary school children with speech disabilities were not given the special instruction they receive today. Ernie's reaction to his speech problem was characteristically courageous, and set a pattern of behavior he was to follow in confronting other problems later in life. By sheer persistence and ingenuity he made remarkable progress in mastering his speech difficulty to the extent that many who came to know him later in life were never aware that he had had a speech problem.

His ultimate success was remarkable in that his disability was apparently quite serious in childhood. Chuck Davis told about how he had to act almost as an interpreter for Ernie when they were children. "We'd be playing," he explained, "and then there would be an argument. The kids would ask Ernie what he thought, but instead of answering, he would wait until I spoke and then just point at me and nod in agreement." One can easily imagine the agonies of embarrassment the young boy must have suffered in school when asked questions in class or otherwise called on to perform in public. Chuck Davis recalled that on his report cards teachers would comment that Ernie did his lessons well but that he never asked any questions. Chuck also recalled humorous aspects of Ernie's childhood stuttering problem. The Davis boys played in the woods near their house. A favorite trick was to run along the trail and snap a sapling back on those behind. One day Chuck snapped it back on Ernie who fell to the ground crying. Since he had never seen Ernie cry before, Chuck assumed he was badly hurt. Not wanting to be punished he ran home first and told his mother Ernie had fallen out of a tree and hurt himself. Shortly Ernie came slowly walking down the street crying and holding his wrist. With all the excitement his appearance caused, he was only able to stutter "tree" so everybody assumed he had fallen out of a tree as Chuck had said. Even after the commotion subsided he never did tell the true story of what had happened much to Chuck's relief.

Another episode concerned a potentially disasterous swimming session at a local pool. Since neither of the boys could swim, their mother signed them up for lessons at the YMCA. At the first lesson the boys had to practice kicking while holding on to the side of the pool. "My hands slipped and I went under," Chuck remembered. "I grabbed Ernie's legs to save myself and pulled him under. Ernie kept bobbing to the surface and I kept pulling him back down. Finally he stuttered out the word drown which alerted the lifeguard and caused him to pull us out. Afterward Ernie said 'We're never going back in that pool again.' We were afraid to tell mom so we went to the Y each week but we never did go swimming again."

Chuck gave insights into how Ernie learned to cope with his handicap and eventually to overcome it. During their younger years, Ernie would read aloud from his school books or sports books until he could pronounce every word without hesitation. The habit of reading contributed also to his confidence as he began to realize that he knew more than others on many subjects of discussion in school and at home. He reached the point where he relished debate, at least with friends and family. Chuck said Ernie's rule in debate was that you can't argue about facts, only about opinions. And his knowledge of the facts made him a formidable opponent for any who tried to get the better of him by mere force of assertion.

After his award-winning senior year in college, he was in great demand on the sports banquet circuit, where he had to make speeches before hundreds of strangers. As in other aspects of his life, when Ernie found something he initially couldn't do, he worked on improving himself. Before making a speech, he would write key words on a small piece of paper and practice before a mirror with a tape recorder, avoiding the words that caused him problems.

Although by the time he reached college few were aware of his speech difficulties, he continued to work quietly and doggedly to improve his speech. Aware of what he was doing, Chuck would sometimes tease him and ask him to pronounce a particularly difficult word. Ernie would often not rise to the bait, but would simply assert that he could pronounce the word. Then some weeks later Chuck would get a telephone call and the first sound he would hear would be the word in question followed by Ernie's laughter in the background. "I told you I could say it," Ernie would boast.

The youthful embarrassment Ernie suffered as a result of his speech problems may have helped to nurture another character trait—compassion. Everyone mentioned this aspect of his character. According to Chuck, he never criticized anyone, and when others did, he always defended the person under attack. From bitter experience he was aware that people who appeared "different" were sometimes unable to help themselves. Chuck recalled that whenever anyone was being teased, Ernie would defend them saying, "Leave him alone. Nobody likes to be embarrassed."

Because of his size and general air of maturity, Ernie was often regarded as older by other boys, including his Uncle Chuck. Chuck would ask his mother, "He's really older than we are, isn't he? You're just not telling us." Yet despite his physical advantages, Ernie was never aggressive. He was a peace maker with his playmates, avoided fights when he could, and was revulsed by cruelty. Chuck recalled an occasion when the boys shot and killed a bird with a BB gun. Ernie was upset and buried the bird with sadness. He refused to play with the BB gun again, and the other boys, also eventually stopped.

Ernie was a competitive athlete, but he believed that games were to be played for fun. One afternoon during a pickup football game between a team of blacks and a team of whites, an opponent kept hitting Ernie in the head. His teammates urged him to stop the battering by retaliating, but Ernie demurred, saying the culprit just didn't know how to play any differently. Later the dirty player tried again, but Ernie ducked at the last instant, throwing the would-be tackler hard on the ground. Furious, he jumped up and punched Ernie, who then retaliated. "We were all happy," said Chuck, "but Ernie walked away, saying, 'It's just a game. It isn't any fun anymore.' "

Chuck repeatedly talked of Ernie's feelings for others.

One incident that impressed him deeply concerned a particularly vigorous display of affection for Chuck on Ernie's part. The two boys went on a Boy Scout outing a few miles outside Uniontown. The scoutmaster went to get supplies and left Ernie in charge. Chuck, disappointed over not being selected leader, hitchhiked back to Uniontown without telling anyone. Upon realizing Chuck was missing a distraught Ernie organized a search. Obviously it was unsuccessful. The scoutmaster had to physically put Ernie in the car and take him back to Uniontown telling him that Chuck was probably already there.

They dropped Ernie—still distraught—at a corner, but instead of going home he waited hoping Chuck would appear. His older uncle, Willie Davis, five years his senior, asked him what he was doing. Ernie explained how he had lost Chuck. Willie informed him that Chuck had been home for hours and that he was playing basketball at the playground.

Ernie ran over to the playground and there was Chuck. As the elder Davis vividly recalled, "Ernie charged onto the court and yanked me up by the shirt. He just kept shaking me back and forth. He was crying and didn't say anything. I was so scared I didn't dare say anything. Finally he dropped me and just walked away. I never did anything like that again."

Ernie's sensitivity to others was illustrated by an incident recounted by Kay Lockwood, a Syracuse University graduate student in 1961, in a letter to the sports editor of *The New York Times* in November 1980. One Friday evening, she said, she and a friend were the only women eating in the university dining hall used by the football team. The players, exuberant and raucous, were vividly describing the impending fate of Saturday's opponent, using obscenities liberally. Lockridge wrote, "Davis got up and quietly reminded his teammates there were women present. No one challenged or argued with Davis. The men continued to discuss what they were going to do to the other team the next day—without the four-letter words and phrases that had peppered the earlier comments. I thanked Davis on my way out. He smiled and said, 'forget it.' I never have—nor have I forgotten him."

A sense of humor was an integral part of Ernie's personality. Everyone referred to his "great laugh and sense of humor." He never took himself too seriously and enjoyed stories about himself. Jack Moore said, "He had a delightful sense of humor. When something funny happened to him that would be embarrassing, he'd love to tell that kind of story. He'd never tell you about being an All-American."

His practical jokes were subtle and pixyish. Once Moore, who attended a nearby college, called Ernie for a student ticket to a sold-out Syracuse game. At the last minute he was able to secure a ticket and a student I.D. for Moore. For admission to the stadium, a student had to give his ticket and show his I.D. During halftime Moore, bespectacled, and white, checked the I.D. Ernie had given him. It belonged to John Brown, a black tackle on the football team. Recalled Moore, "I knew Ernie was down on the field chuckling to himself wondering whether or not I got in with that I.D. card."

A favorite family story was told by Chuck Davis. The two boys had just been given new winter hats and were sent to the grocery store. On the way they stopped by Chuckle Run, a stream where a rope was tied to the limb of a tree enabling the kids to swing back and forth from bank to bank. On Ernie's last swing, his new hat fell into the stream and was being swept away by the current. Aghast, he swung down into the stream to retrieve his hat. As Chuck recounted with a laugh, "He was running so fast through the water he never got his feet wet."

The uncle recalled how Ernie would tease him when they were adults about something that occurred when they were children. Chuck had been afraid of the dark as a kid, so they had slept with the light on in the bedroom they shared. Chuck recalled, "Whenever we got together later and slept in the same room, he would always leave the light on without ever saying a word. It was sort of a gentle leg-pulling."

Ernie was also the butt of jokes, an indication that others viewed him as good natured and able to enjoy even humor turned against him. One of his former teammates recalled such a practical joke involving Ernie's famous number 44 football jersey. Before his final home game at Archbold Stadium, someone hid the jersey. The Syracuse equipment manager was Al Zak, who ruled his domain so fiercely that the athletes dreaded approaching him if they lost equipment. With no exceptions, you turned in your equipment how and when Zak said. If you turned in only one sock, you got only one sock in return.

Just prior to leaving the locker room for pregame warm-ups, a visibly nervous Ernie said to Bill Fitzgerald, "I can't find my jersey." He was frantically looking all around. Fitzgerald suggested, "Go ask Zak for another one." Ernie responded, "I can't do that!" Fitzgerald asked, "What are you going to do, not play today?" Ernie began searching more frantically and asking others if they had seen his jersey. Finally, the perpetrators felt the joke had gone far enough and someone "found" the jersey.

Chuck recalled another episode in which Ernie, if not the butt of the joke, was at least an unwilling subject. It concerned Ernie's penchant for buying clothes in New York's garment district whenever he was there visiting relatives who had moved to Brooklyn from Uniontown. Chuck Davis recalled, "Ernie liked this one particular shop. I told him the tailor was gay, although he really wasn't. Ernie would get really nervous whenever the tailor started to measure him. I'd always get the tailor to measure the trouser inseam a couple of times. Ernie would look at me and shake his head."

The story of Ernie's childhood would not be complete without noting the influences that pushed him toward a career in sports. First of all, his uncles provided role models in this field. Willie Davis, the older uncle, was the first in the family to excel in sports, and Chuck followed close behind. Moreover, the neighborhood was a hot bed of athletic talent. Games such as football, basketball, softball and track, were always being organized. As Ernie wrote in

The Saturday Evening Post magazine article, "We pretty much lived on the playgrounds. Sports were the only recreation we had. Nothing seemed as important to us as succeeding in sports."

The western Pennsylvania coal mining region had a strong athletic tradition and was particularly well known to college football recruiters. Notre Dame, Heisman Trophy winner Johnny Lujack and baseball Hall of Famer Stan Musial were from nearby. One of Ernie's childhood playmates, Sandy Stephens, became an All-American football player at the University of Minnesota and finished fourth behind Ernie in the Heisman Trophy balloting in 1961. Another Uniontown athlete of that time was Bill Munsey who also starred at Minnesota. Munsey's brothers Nelson and Chuck became professional stars with the Baltimore Colts and San Diego Chargers respectively. Chuck spells his name differently but he is indeed a brother of the other two.

Sports have always been a big part of a boy's life in America, but in Uniontown they were everything. It is not surprising that in describing his childhood, Ernie recalled an episode involving sports as his most unforgettable experience. He and his friend Sandy Stephens, joined the Uniontown Midget Baseball League as eight-year olds and tried out for the Benson's team because it had uniforms similar to the Brooklyn Dodgers. Up to this time, neither child had ever worn a uniform. He set a goal of wearing one of the team's fifteen uniforms in the midget league parade through Uniontown that opened the season. At the final team cut, the coach told Ernie he was the final player on the team.

Always punctual, he arrived early for the parade. But when the uniforms were passed out, he did not receive one. In describing his feelings Ernie wrote, "I couldn't believe it. I kept standing around trying not to cry. Finally the parade took off. I can still see the way they looked, marching up the street, marching up the street and out of sight without me. It was my first big disappointment in sports. Not many have hurt that much, and while it seems amusing now, I still can understand how I felt."

Such individual disappointment was rare for Ernie, however, because early in his sports career he began to demonstrate the abilities that made him a clutch performer. Throughout his All-American high school and college careers, coaches and fans alike remembered him as always coming through in the important games.

Ernie honed the "clutch" skill from his earliest days on the playgrounds of Uniontown. Among his playmates he was the best athlete in every sport. Chuck recalled, "We always expected him to win the game. We'd shout, 'Come on Ernie, you can do it. Come on Ernie, you got to do it.' He did it."

Curiously, the boys concentrated on basketball as they grew older because their parents became opposed to football after a local high school player died in a game. They started out on a dirt court near home, shoveling the snow off during the winter. They soon moved up to the playgrounds in Uniontown. Ernie became a high school All-American. Chuck became a three-time NAIA All American at Westminister College and tried out for the 1960 United States Olympic Team.

All three of the Davis boys earned extra money caddying at the local country club and also learned how to play golf. Willie was old enough and strong enough for the job. The diminutive Chuck had difficulty carrying two heavy golf bags. Ernie who wasn't old enough to caddy would hide at the third hole. When Chuck arrived there he would take over carrying the clubs until the 17th hole where Chuck took over again. Chuck would get paid and then split the money with Ernie.

The highlight of each summer for Ernie and Chuck was going to see professional baseball games. Their father was an avid baseball fan and took them to see the Homestead Grays of the Negro Baseball League. Everybody's hero was the legendary catcher, Josh Gibson. Ernie's favorite player, however, was Buck Leonard, the first baseman. When

Jackie Robinson of the Brooklyn Dodgers broke the color barrier in major league baseball, their father took them to Forbes Field in Pittsburgh to watch him play. Ever after they regarded the Dodger's as "their" team.

When he was 12 years old, Ernie's life changed dramatically as he moved from his grandparents home to live permanently with his mother and stepfather in Elmira, New York. Ernie had become such an accepted and integral part of the Davis family that most neighbors did not know he wasn't a son until he moved. He was not enthusiastic about moving and leaving his family and friends because, like most children, he thought making new ones would be impossible. His grandmother ended all discussion by saying, "Ernie, you have to go." The family bond his grandparents forged remained strong however, and Ernie visited them often in later years.

Elmira

The move, although initially upsetting, gave Ernie opportunities he would not have had in Uniontown. He came under the influence of such men as Tony DeFilippo, Marty Harrigan, and Jim Flynn, who guided him in his athletic career and later gave him the benefit of their experience in his business and personal affairs.

Ernie became an Elmira sports legend as a two-time, two-sport high school All-American. By his senior year, recruiters from across the country were vying for his athletic services. In that more innocent time, Ernie's and the teams' success, particularly in basketball, united the student body and the community. As a result of his sports celebrity, he became one of Elmira's best-known ambassadors to the nation.

Elmira is an industrial community on the Chemung River just over the Pennsylvania state line in the southern tier of New York. World famous tourist attractions like the Finger Lakes and Watkins Glen are nearby. Elmira College houses the study of author Mark Twain, who wrote *Tom Sawyer* and worked on other novels, while living in the area after marrying Olivia Langdon of Elmira. In the early 1950s, Elmira was a city of approximately 50,000 but retained many characteristics of a small town surrounded by rural area. Influenced more by Pennsylvania than New

York, the city was keyed to a more leisurely pace than other New York cities of comparable size.

Since school was not in session and Ernie was a shy youngster in a new city, it was difficult for him to make friends initially. After several weeks, sports once again provided Ernie with an outlet. He joined the Superior Buick team in the city's Small Fry Football League. To reduce injuries, the league had weight restrictions for each position. The bigger boys were linemen and the smaller ones backs. Ernie wanted to play halfback, but because of his size, he had to play tackle. He never complained, for he was happy just to be playing.

Physically and emotionally mature at a young age, Ernie never tried to embarrass or intimidate a less gifted opponent. Later in high school, many people would recall how Ernie would hold back against inferior teams rather than run up his personal totals.

Once during a Small Fry game, instead of slamming a 75-pound quarterback to the ground, Ernie just picked him up and held him. When the whistle blew, he put the boy back down on his feet. Ernie was confident enough of his athletic ability, even at that age, to realize he didn't have to smash an opponent to be recognized. His concern for others extended to the athletic field. His reputation was never going to be made at the expense of less gifted athletes.

The Superior Buick team went on to a championship, and Ernie became a Small Fry All-Star in both 1952 and 1953. It was the first of many honors and awards he would win in Elmira and throughout the country. He also established a friendship that later in his career proved to be beneficial. Teammate Ted DeFilippo's mother organized team picnics at her house. There, Ernie met Ted's father, Tony DeFilippo, who became his lawyer and personal advisor.

In addition to football, Ernie continued to play basketball, just as he had in Uniontown. His initial basketball success in Elmira was at the Neighborhood House where he became a grade school all-star. The Neighborhood House was similar to a settlement house, and he spent a great deal of time there while growing up. While in high school he coached there and later visited when he was in town. When Ernie entered high school in 1954, his reputation from the Small Fry League and the Neighborhood House preceded him. The coaches at Elmira Free Academy High School (EFA), which was directly across the street from Ernie's home, looked forward to his arrival. Their anticipation was more than justified by his performance over the next four years: eleven varsity letters in three sports, unbeaten championship teams in football and basketball, and numerous personal awards.

A combination of attributes made Ernie a superior athlete in high school. His football coach, Marty Harrigan, put it succinctly. "Talent is important, but dependability is critical. You take talent and intensity, put them in one body and you've got a horse."

Harrigan continued, "Ernie Davis was a quiet leader, not the rah-rah guy, but the leader who does it by example. He was very humble, extremely popular with his peers and respected by the faculty." The coach recalled a time when prior to an important game, he gave an impassioned locker room speech and sent the team flying out the door. Glancing back he saw Ernie helping a scrub who had put his shoulder pads on incorrectly. He made sure they were tight, and they ran out on the field together.

Varsity basketball coach Jim Flynn said, "Ernie was the leader and he actually made everybody better than they were. The team played up to his standards instead of going their own way. They realized they had something to live up to with him."

One of the many things that set Ernie apart in an athletic contest was his ability to respond under pressure. Harrigan described it. "When the score is 36-6, he played like just another player. When the score is 13-12 or 6-6 in the last quarter, look out. Talk about rising to the occasion. Anybody can play when its a slaughter." Flynn said, "When the chips were down and the going was tough, Ernie was always there. Every time. I never saw a guy like him. He came through every single time."

Despite his later achievements, Ernie's high school athletic career did not begin auspiciously. His freshman football year was short lived. Playing end in the first minute of the first jayvee game of the year, Ernie again broke his right wrist and was sidelined the entire season.

The injury postponed an assessment of Ernie's football skills. Instead it was through basketball that Harrigan first gauged Ernie's athletic potential. "We realized," said Harrigan, "what kind of athletic talent he had—gifted, balance, agility—by watching him play basketball that first year."

His football career blossomed his sophomore year when Ernie became a two-way starter at end. The experience of playing end initially in high school and tackle in the Small Fry League aided Ernie's development as a football player. Rather than just being a gifted runner he first learned the fundamentals of blocking, tackling and receiving which enabled him to become an all-around rather than a one dimensional player. Harrigan recalled, "On defense, he had great hands. He was also a good blocker."

With all his physical gifts, Ernie still had trouble with pushups during this stage of his career. He had thick hips and long gangly arms. This inspired college teammates John Brown and John Mackey to call him "Bubbles." Harrigan said, "I remember so well the other kids kidding him about his inability to do a pushup right. He'd push his fanny up and then his front up, then he'd go the other way, push his front up and then try to get his fanny up. I can see him doing it now."

Ernie worked on this shortcoming, as he had his stutter, and developed the upper body strength necessary to do pushups. "Just a simple thing," said Harrigan, "but even something as simple as that he worked at. I think it's indicative of drive and wanting to do things right. Some guys can't do these things, so they let it go at that."

Although aware of Ernie's outstanding running ability, coach Harrigan did not switch him from end to halfback immediately. "We probably ran more end arounds that season than most coaches do in a lifetime," the coach said. However, halfway through his junior season, due to injuries in the backfield, Ernie was switched to halfback. The Blue Devils went on to finish the season undefeated and win the league championship.

Ernie's performances at halfback began to attract the attention of college recruiters from around the country. However, Syracuse University coach Ben Schwartzwalder, tipped off by area alumni about an "outstanding prospect in Elmira", had been following Ernie since his sophomore year. The alumni assistance and the early jump on the competition would prove crucial in his eventual recruitment of Ernie.

With a season at halfback, Ernie improved on the potential he had shown as a junior. He became the first high-school football player in Elmira to average 100 yards per game for an entire season. Perhaps his best game was against Southside of Elmira, when he scored twice on runs of over 90 yards. The Blue Devils were once again undefeated as the end of the season approached. Prior to an important game with Vestal, the team was decimated by the Asian Flu. Ernie, not stricken, was at his competitive best, but the team was badly beaten. They also lost the following week to Binghamton Central, but Ernie was once again all over the field. Appreciating his effort, the admiring Central fans gave him a standing ovation.

Awards and honors for Ernie were commonplace at the conclusion of each season. In all three of his varsity seasons, Ernie was chosen first team All Southern Tier Conference. As a junior and a senior, he was both Elmira Player of the Year and high-school All-American.

His career offensive statistics included: 1,314 yards rushing on 179 carries for a 7.4 yard average per attempt. He completed 13 passes for 240 yards and caught 27 for 516 yards. Ernie scored 21 touchdowns and kicked 12 extra points. All this was done while playing half his high-school career at end. Coach Harrigan summarized, "You can't coach the instinct and the moves he had. All you can do is encourage him and use him in the proper way."

As successful as he was in football, Ernie's high school basketball career was even more memorable. He led EFA to a 52-game victory streak and two successive sectional championships. Ironically early in his career, many, including his mother, believed Ernie would concentrate on basketball rather than football. His first varsity athletic achievements in high school were as a freshman on the basketball team.

Ernie's wrist was still in a cast from the jayvee football injury when he attended varsity basketball practice for the first time. The Blue Devils coach Bill Wipfler told Ernie he couldn't play with the cast. Ernie continued to attend practice, and finally the coach relented, since Ernie was 6 feet and 175 pounds.

With his wrist heavily bandaged, Ernie entered the first game of the season against Union-Endicott midway through the first quarter. He scored 22 points and became a regular for the remainder of his high-school career. At season's end, he was honorable mention all-conference.

Coach Jim Flynn became varsity basketball coach during Ernie's sophomore year and naturally brought a change in basketball philosophy. Everyone, including Ernie, told the new coach he was good within ten feet of the basket, but was ineffective farther out. Flynn recalled, "I didn't want him near the basket if I could help it."

The new coach had never seen Ernie play, but had been told about his great athletic skill. At their first meeting early in the school year, the coach told Ernie he wanted to move him away from the basket. Flynn remembered, "Ernie said, 'I'll do anything you want me to do'. That was characteristic of his attitude all the way through. He was the hardest worker you ever saw in anything. Just super." Unlike many kids with great physical talent, Ernie was always coachable right through college. He believed in team work and would do anything the coaches wanted to benefit the team.

The coach instructed Ernie in the technique of the two-hand set shot and driving either the baseline or back to the center of the court. Said Flynn, "Right from the start of practice, I kept him every night, and we worked on his set shot and drives." Ernie also came to the gym before practice and worked on his technique. By the beginning of the season his hard work paid off, and he mastered both.

The season's opener was against crosstown rival Southside at the Elmira Armory. Southside played a zone defense and dropped off Ernie, because based on past performance, they didn't think he could shoot from the outside. Flynn recalled, "He hit three set shots right in a row. They called time out. Ernie came over and said, 'They think I can't shoot from the outside.' He was highly insulted. It wasn't his style. He wasn't that sort of guy, but I think it just sort of hurt his pride for them to think they could lay off him and get away with it."

As in football, Ernie was a leader by example. Before each game a tradition developed, which continued for the remainder of Ernie's career at EFA. In the pre-game huddle, he always led the team in the Lord's Prayer. Flynn said, "It wasn't anything set up. Nothing was ever said. He just did it."

The basketball team had a number of football players in addition to Ernie and got off to a slow start his sophomore year. Over Christmas they began to jell and won fourteen games in a row. In the last game of the season EFA lost at Cortland, 57–55, in the final of the state section four playoffs. It was the last high school basketball game Ernie ever lost.

During his junior and senior years the Blue Devils were undefeated winning 52 games in a row which was a New York state record until Lew Alcindor (now Kareem Abdul-Jabbar) and his Power Memorial teammates broke it in the 1960's. In his final 67 high school basketball games Ernie led EFA to a 66–1 record. His junior year was also Ernie's

most productive from a scoring standpoint as he totaled
540 points.

Because of the pounding he had taken during the football season, the success of Ernie's final basketball campaign
appeared in doubt. He had a severe lower back pain that
restricted his lateral movement. Players who were later cut
were driving past him with no difficulty. Coach Flynn
remembered, "I found a drill in a basketball magazine to
loosen up the back and legs. After using it for a few weeks,
Ernie's back began to respond. He had been scared. When
it came around, he was the same old Ernie, big smile,
everything great, let's go."

Ernie was confident but never cocky. Before his final
basketball season, he had a conversation with teammate
Jack Moore, now a lawyer in Elmira. Moore related, "I said,
wouldn't it be something if we could go undefeated again?
I remember thinking we can't do that again. But Ernie
answered, 'We will. We can do that again.' He thought we
could and we did."

In his final game against Southside at the Elmira Armory, Ernie's performance was one coach Flynn will never
forget. Ernie had set an intra-city scoring record of 36
points against them and had never lost to Southside during his basketball career. Southside's star player on the
other hand, had never had an outstanding game against
EFA. The Blue Devils had the game under control before
5,000 fans when the Southside star went on a scoring binge
with five or six baskets in succession. Coach Flynn was
certain of the reason but verified it with Ernie.

"You let him go at the end, Ernie," the coach asserted.
Ernie responded, "Coach, I've played against him for three
years. I like him, he's a friend. They never give him the ball
and he's good. I thought if I stayed off him enough they
would have to give him the ball and he could get some
points." Flynn concluded, "The guy got a little write-up in
the paper on his scoring. Ernie and I were the only ones
who knew why."

In basketball, as in football, Ernie was always at his best

in the important games. Against lesser opponents, he would purposely play a less significant role in the contest. In the play-offs against a strong team from Vestal, Ernie wanted to ensure the Blue Devils got off to a fast start, so he scored the first six times down the court. "Whenever a threat came against a good team, he was unbelievable," Flynn recalled. "People have an offnight, but not him. He just came through. He could rise to the occasion."

Teammate Moore said, "When the going got rough, you went to him. You could just tell he wanted the ball. I wanted to give it to him too. Against the tough teams he had the best statistics—25 points and 15 rebounds. He'd have fewer points but more assists against a team that really wasn't that good."

The effect of the basketball team's victory skein was felt by his family, the student body and the community. Despite the mounting pressure of each game, Ernie showed no reaction to the streak. His mother recalled, "He was very competitive. Whether he had a good game or a bad game, his mood didn't seem to change. I really don't know why, modesty, I guess." Arthur Radford, Ernie's stepfather, worked the midnight shift at the Corning Glass Works factory in Corning, New York, several miles northwest of Elmira. On his way home in the morning, he would purchase the newspaper and read about the basketball games. When he arrived home, Ernie would be waking up for school. Radford recalled, "Ernie'd wake up singing and go to bed singing. I'd ask about the game and he'd say 'We won.' He never talked about himself. That's why I bought the newspaper."

Ernie remained close to Radford even after his mother divorced him. Radford recollected, "Even after we broke up whenever he came to town, he'd always come by and take me to dinner. His mother didn't know where I was, so I don't know how he found out, but he always did." Coach Flynn said, "He was respected by everybody in the school. The school was better because of this man. The whole student body was uplifted by one guy. They just adored the guy." During Ernie's recruitment, Syracuse coach Ben Schwartzwalder was most impressed by a visit to EFA's principal, who told him, "Ben, he [Ernie] is the finest school citizen we ever had in Elmira, and I never expect to find another one equal to him." The Elmira City Council passed a resolution honoring the team and Ernie after the season.

Perhaps Elmira's reaction was best summarized by a father who eventually realized that for some time his young son had been drinking an inordinate amount of chocolate milk. When asked why, the boy replied, "I want to be like Ernie Davis."

By season's end, Ernie had broken the all-time Southern Tier Conference career scoring record with 1,605 points for an 18.4 average during 87 varsity games. He was unanimous all-conference pick his sophomore, junior and senior years as well as Elmira Player of the Year the same three seasons. He was the conference tournament MVP in his junior year. As in football, he was a two-time All-American. The capstone to Ernie's scholastic athletic career in his junior and senior years, was being selected the Elmira Athlete of the Year both years.

His coach, Jim Flynn and teammate Jack Moore both agreed the success of the basketball team was attributable to Ernie's efforts. There was obviously good material and good coaching, but Ernie was the key. "You could take somebody else out, but you couldn't take Ernie out of there," stated Moore. "He was the only one who couldn't be replaced. You couldn't have done it without him." Ernie ended each high school year by earning a letter playing varsity baseball. His first year he was a pitcher and his last three seasons, a first baseman with great defensive skills. He was a left-handed batter with a .300 average who could hit for power. Although Ernie always felt baseball was the weakest of his three major sports, at least one professional scout had another opinion.

One afternoon at Dunn Field, some scouts were sitting behind home plate when Ernie lined a drive off the fence.

One of them remarked, "Harness that power, correct that swing a little, and this boy could be a major leaguer. He's got everything else, size, speed, and a throwing arm."

Ernie believed he was fortunate to be so gifted and never took his ability for granted. He worked tirelessly to improve. A defeat due to improper conditioning would be anathema to him. He always worked hard in all aspects of practice. As former EFA and Syracuse teammate Bill Fitzgerald said, "Ernie was always the first one on the practice field and the last to leave. He finished first in running laps and wind sprints." Late in the summer, just before football practice began, some players would go over to Parker Field to work out. On arrival, they would find Ernie had already been there working out for weeks.

Being such a gifted athlete from a small town, Ernie received tremendous local newspaper coverage. Stories and pictures about his exploits appeared continuously. Ernie had the self-confidence and humility not to be affected by media attention. "He got the greatest write-ups you ever saw from a small town like this," said Coach Flynn. "He handled it so easily. It's something that even as an adult, I could never have handled. Some kids get stories about them printed and they think they're the greatest. Nobody has ever heard of them yet. Ernie was the same kid at the end he was at the start."

In high school Ernie's influence extended beyond the athletic field and into the classroom. Many teenagers with his athletic skill, assured of a college scholarship, would have coasted in class and rested on their sports achievements. According to Moore, "Ernie worked hard when it wasn't popular to work hard to get good grades. It was easier for me to work hard and get good grades because he was there. He made it okay to do that." Coach Flynn recalled, "The teachers loved him. He never would excuse himself from work and say he had too many outside activities."

Despite his basketball success, Ernie decided to concentrate on football his senior year. "I don't know why he

Jump shot during varsity high school action, 1957 (Courtesy Al Mallette)

chose football," his mother said. "I guess he just liked it better". Although he never articulated his reasons, certainly the influence of Marty Harrigan was important. Elmira sports editor Al Mallette thought Ernie concentrated on football in college rather than basketball because the latter was being dominated by big men. Mallette opined, "Ernie was only 6'2" and would have had to been a guard in college. He had played only forward and center in high school. His game was not geared to playing guard."

Six weeks before he died Ernie described his feelings about football in *The Saturday Evening Post*.

A lot of things go into it, the excitement, the physical contact, the skill, the crowds. But the big thing to me in football has always been the competitiveness. Sometimes when the game is close and the play is the roughest, you forget the crowd and the noise, it's just you against somebody else to see who is the better man. This is what I liked and took pride in. . .

At the conclusion of Ernie's senior football season, scholarship offers from over 50 colleges, coast to coast, including Notre Dame, Air Force, and UCLA were received. Some athletes today receive hundreds of offers, but in 1958, recruiting was not as sophisticated as it is today, and many colleges particularly those in the South, did not offer scholarships to black athletes. At Syracuse University, head football coach, Ben Schwartzwalder, prepared to launch a massive recruiting effort for the prospect 90 miles south in Elmira.

Schwartzwalder said, "You see a good one run one time and you know. He had reflexes, speed, size and strength. Then add to that the fact he is such a great person and you couldn't miss. I don't know how many schools were after him, everybody who played football, I guess. If it weren't for Tony DeFilippo and Marty Harrigan, we wouldn't have had a chance at all."

DeFilippo and Harrigan were Syracuse alumni and extremely close to Ernie. During Ernie's final two years in high school, Schwartzwalder made approximately 30 trips to Elmira and on each occasion saw Ernie. He recalled, "We were pretty well acquainted by the time he got here." The informal meetings were usually held at DeFilippo's house.

Ernie's main requirement was a good education, which would prepare him for the future. He intended to play professional football, but knew the career expectancy for running backs in the NFL was only a few seasons, so he wanted to be prepared for another career when he retired from football. The coach stressed academics in his visits, "Football is giving you an opportunity to get an education. Get it. In football you might never make it. What you have in your mind, nobody is going to take away from you." Initially Ernie was leaning toward Notre Dame and the Air

Force Academy. A number of factors influenced his eventual selection of Syracuse. It was close to home, enabling his mother and others an opportunity to watch him play. Other blacks had played there, done well, and been accepted. The team was winning and the influence of De-Filippo and Harrigan helped. "We knew those people at Syracuse," Harrigan stated. "We could get on the phone and find out how things were going. Out on the coast, we didn't know those people and wouldn't see them again. It did work out fine, thank God."

Because of his ability, Ernie's decision was significant for him as well as others. Prior to making his commitment, Ernie sought advice. His uncle, Chuck Davis, had been heavily recruited two years earlier for basketball. Chuck had decided to attend small Westminster College rather than accept an offer from a larger school. They discussed the pros and cons. Finally, Ernie told Chuck, "Exposure is half the battle of education and helps you learn. I'm going to a large school because I'll be exposed to more."

Jim Brown had been an All-American at Syracuse and had just begun his legendary career as fullback for the Cleveland Browns. Schwartzwalder scheduled to speak at an awards luncheon in Elmira honoring Ernie, asked Brown to accompany him. The coach's plan was to have Brown talk to Ernie about attending Syracuse. The crush of the crowd seeking autographs was so great that the coach was unable to get the two football players together privately. In desperation just before they left, Brown was able to get his arm around Ernie and say, "Go to Syracuse."

Brown and Schwartzwalder drove back to Syracuse together, and the coach remembered part of their conversation. "Jim said, 'Coach, I never saw so many people. I didn't have a chance to talk to Ernie.'" Schwartzwalder recalled thanking Jim for his effort," If you could only say three words, you couldn't think of three better ones—'Go to Syracuse.' " At the time, Brown was neither Ernie's idol nor friend. The two became closer, however, after Ernie graduated from Syracuse and signed with the Cleveland Browns.

After making campus visits, Ernie and his mother discussed them. When the discussions were over, Ernie was permitted to make the final choice. His mother recalled, "One day he said, "I've made up my mind. I want to go to Syracuse.' I said, if that's what you want, that's what you do."

Ernie was later quoted in the newspapers as saying of the recruiting period, "I had a lot of people talking to me. But I guess they knew from the start where I was going. Once I thought I would like to go to Notre Dame, but I figured I might get lost in the shuffle. Syracuse is close to home." His mother, his coaches, and others drove the 90 miles to Syracuse to watch him play.

Ernie was fiercely loyal and never forgot the people and the places that influenced his career. Ernie accompanied Syracuse Coach Ben Schwartzwalder to Floyd Little's house on a recruiting trip in December 1962. Little said, "He romanced my mother, flirted with my three sisters, and didn't say much to me. He was the type who overhelmed you with his presence. He said, 'Besides football, it will give you an opportunity to get an education. Besides that, they haven't discovered the forward pass and it's a great place if you want to carry the ball a lot.'" Upon hearing of Ernie's death, Little called Schwartzwalder and said, "I'm coming." Little eventually added to the University's football tradition by also wearing number 44 and breaking Ernie's rushing records.

After the pressure of making his college selection and graduating from high school, Ernie looked forward to his summer vacation in 1958: a highlight was his selection to play in the first high school sectional All-Star game in Binghamton, New York. Practice was held for a week at a camp where a lake served as the bathing facility.

After their first practice, the other players eagerly dived into the lake while Ernie paced warily back and forth on the dock asking if the water was deep. Knowing he couldn't swim, his teammates directed him to another part of the dock where they said the water was shallow. Trustingly, Ernie leaped in. The water was over his head. After flailing away for a few seconds, he was rescued. When he caught his breath on the dock Ernie said, "I'm getting a bucket and washing on the shore for the rest of the week."

Despite all of Ernie's athletic achievements, it is as a person, not an athlete, that his friends from high school remember him. Jack Moore recalled, "He would always make you feel good about being around him. He was more concerned about me than he was about himself if the two of us were talking. He was the type of person you'd like your kids to be like. He was the type of person you'd like yourself to be like. I never met anybody like him. He wanted to make other people feel good."

Bill Fitzgerald, now Dean of Students at Elmira Free Academy said, "He had the qualities people in education would like to see in all the kids we deal with—honesty, integrity, responsibility, self-direction and sense of community. You just wanted to be around him. He was honest with everybody. He didn't say one thing out of one side of his mouth and then do something else."

Ernie's two high-school coaches who have spent their careers working with young people, independently summed up their feelings with the same word and the same conclusion. Marty Harrigan said "He's the type of person that when he walked into a room. . .people looked. There was something about him. He was something special."

Jim Flynn stated, "He was a man when he was a boy. This guy had done everything, and you wouldn't even know he was around except for his presence. He was a dominating figure without trying to be one. He raised all of us up. Made all of us better than we were and that includes myself. You couldn't be around him without feeling it. He was just special."

In the lobby of the Elmira Free Academy High School is a large publicity photograph of Ernie from his Syracuse University playing days. A plaque next to the photo details Ernie's athletic accomplishments at EFA and Syracuse. The inscription summarizes, "He could do it all, beat every opponent . . . except one."

Syracuse

When Ernie enrolled at Syracuse University in the fall of 1958, college life was in the waning period of a socially and politically complacent time. Then the big events on campus were panty raids and pep rallies. Most of the students were from the upper income families and viewed their college life as an interlude, unrelated to the real life that would follow. In many cases future careers had already been mapped out and the college degree was seen as a necessary step in preparing for future professional success.

The campus protests of the late sixties and early seventies over Vietnam, civil rights, the environment and Watergate, which profoundly changed student-administrator relations, were not yet on the horizon. College enrollment in 1960 was less than one third of what it was to become in the early 1980's and it was drawn from a narrower range of social backgrounds. A notable difference in college enrollments concerned women, who were in the minority. An even greater difference concerned blacks, whose numbers on campus have increased five times since the early sixties. When James Meredith became the first black student at the University of Mississippi in 1962, 30,000 federal troops were called up to insure the peace. In Alabama, Governor George Wallace became a national figure when he "stood in the schoolhouse door" to bar blacks from enrolling at the University of Alabama. Despite the broadening of opportunities, black students in the 1960's were aware that their acceptance into the mainstream of American life was at best a provisory one, subject to challenge at any moment.

The social pressure on Ernie and the other black students at Syracuse was enormous. The successful, black, male athletes enjoyed a measure of prestige on the athletic field which was not transfered to daily campus life. Whites seldom faced the need to deal with blacks as individuals or as a group. Blacks, on the other hand, went along to get along. The pressure to conform was very real, even though the rules of conduct were never articulated. John Brown characterized the situation as, "an almost unbearable mental strain."

The subtle barriers facing blacks on campus were no better illustrated than by the virtual non-participation of blacks in the Greek system. Much of the social life for white students revolved around fraternities and sororities. The Greek system on campus was at its zenith. A measure of house prestige was the number of campus celebrities that were members, and the competition among the houses to pledge them was intense. Had Ernie been white, every fraternity on campus would have rushed him. As it was, he was asked by some brothers from Sigma Alpha Mu (Sammy) to rush informally during the fall of 1959.

The complexity of the black and white social issue at Syracuse was exemplified by the internal controversy created within the 'Sammy' brotherhood at the prospect of a black member regardless of his personal popularity. Stanley J. Corwin, a 'Sammy' brother in 1959, wrote an article in the November 2, 1980, *New York Times* about the pledging of Ernie Davis. On the initial straw vote, six hands were raised in opposition. A negative vote by six members barred a prospective pledge. The nays, according to Corwin argued, "He is not our kind. He will not be active in the fraternity and it's hypocritical on our part to pledge a 'name.' Then one of my brothers made an impassioned plea to bar Davis permanently. 'I hope where you come from you've never been attacked or beaten up by niggers. I hope you are ready to lock your personal things up every night and sleep with your wallet under your pillow.' "

In spite of the possible personal consequences, a brother from Rochester demonstrated an uncommon racial tolerance. On the binding vote on Ernie for membership, he lowered his hand previously raised in objection, explaining, "I wanted Ernie Davis to be in the fraternity with all my heart and soul. Otherwise the fraternity didn't mean anything to me at all." Thus he became a member of the fraternity and participated in social functions during the rest of his college career. After his death the brotherhood presented a plaque to his mother in memory of him.

Whatever popularity Ernie enjoyed on campus provided no advantage in the outside world, where he was recognized only as a black. His mother recalled, "He would sit down and tell us about a few racial incidents, but that would be long after they had happened."

Unlike today, a black athlete in the late fifties and early sixties was still a rarity in college athletics. Black athletic advances were measured in one's and two's. Even the northern colleges that admitted blacks did not always do so because of social policy. The University of Alabama, a perennial college football power, did not recruit blacks until 1970.

Sports, which was often ahead of the rest of society in race relations, was still affected by old prejudices. Newspaper sports pages were reporting stories with racial slants. In 1961 black major league baseball players were not registered in the same hotels as white players during spring training. *The Washington Post* columnist Bob Addie wrote in the August 15, 1961 issue:

> The players feel there isn't much more they can do except recommend to the owners that the players be integrated in the Spring camps. "We certainly have proved we can get along fine

with the colored players," says one veteran, "and we're all for
them. But there isn't much we can do about changing the laws.
We'll continue to fight for integration in Spring training but
there's nothing we can do except refuse to play. I'm sure, from
talking to them, that the colored players don't want that kind of
a solution.

On November 29, 1961 the Associated Press reported:

Nine Negro members of San Diego's American League football team said today they had decided to play in Houston
Sunday despite racial segregation of spectators there. Their
statement declared, however, that they had confidence the
league "would take action to eliminate segregation facilities in
all of its cities."

The Associated Press reported on December 30, 1961:

The basketball game between Rhode Island and Oglethorpe
Friday night was an historic event in Georgia intercollegiate
sporting competition.

For the first time, Negro and white patrons shared seating
arrangements at an intercollegiate athletic event. Approximately 20 Negroes sat among the white spectators.

And the capacity crowd gave a resounding ovation to Rhode
Island's Negro star, Charles Lee, when he fouled out in the
second half.

One incident that illustrated black powerlessness at that
time occurred during a college break. Ernie and John
Brown joined a basketball tour organized by a friend of
Ernie's from Elmira. One night they entered a diner outside Baltimore, Maryland, and a waitress refused to serve
them because they were black. Brown reacted, "This is
Ernie Davis, the Heisman Trophy winner." The waitress
replied, "I don't give a damn who he is." Rather than force
the issue, Ernie said, "You can't fight prejudice like that."
They left.

During Ernie's life the civil rights movement was just
beginning to attract national attention. It cannot be said
with absolute certainty how Ernie would have reacted to
the movement. But it seems that a man of Ernie's courage,
with his love for others and deep religious beliefs, would
have been involved. Those who were close to Ernie think
so. Ernie was unequivocally a black man. However, in his
personal social philosophy, he seems to have been non-

racial. He was always more interested in a man's character than his color.

Chuck Davis, active in the NAACP, remembered a conversation he and Ernie had about civil rights.

> I was talking about Martin Luther King, Jr., Malcolm X, and others. He said, that in the future they might be considered 'Uncle Toms' much the same way as Booker T. Washington was considered then. You know he was right. There are some who feel that way now. They are judging them by today's standards which wouldn't have existed without them.

Prejudice was not the only source of social pressure for black athletes. Dating was also difficult because there was a shortage of black coeds. Worse still there was frequently a socio-economic gulf between black coeds and black athletes. The latter were primarily from somewhat culturally and economically deprived backgrounds. On the other hand, black women were frequently from middle class or better backgrounds and were correspondingly better off culturally and financially.

Fall football practice began each year in August before school started and overlapped Freshman Orientation Week. The week before class commenced, freshmen arrived on campus to begin their orientation to campus life. Both black and white players used to attend the scheduled social functions to look at the girls. Mackey recalled one event, "We went to a dance. When we left we went out a side door and down some stairs. Some of the black girls were still lined up to go in when one of them saw us and said to the others, The party must be ready to start, the kitchen help is leaving."

Ernie dated a coed, Helen Gott, who was a year behind him. He also continued to date his girlfriend from Elmira, Betty Snowden. Neither John nor Sylvia Mackey thought the relationship with Helen Gott was serious. However, Sylvia felt, "He liked her more than she liked him."

Initially Ernie went home frequently on weekends and visited Betty Snowden. As time went on Ernie felt they were drifting apart, and this deeply concerned him. He didn't want to give the impression that he felt, because he went to Syracuse University, he was now too good for her or the rest of his old acquaintances and friends in Elmira. John Mackey remembered his talking about this dilemma. Mackey said, "I'd tell him, 'I can understand your being concerned about the girl's feelings, but not the whole town's. You can't worry about what the whole town thinks.' But he did."

The black athletes were caught in a "Catch 22" situation. There was great pressure to perform academically and athletically. Success in either area was seen as a potential springboard to economic success. However, the more successful one became as a student or particularly as an athlete, the more one found himself under critical scrutiny.

Another form of social pressure was applied by those blacks who felt it was important not to rock the boat. They felt the athletes had a tremendous opportunity and also a responsibility for those who hopefully would come later. This was manifest at Syracuse by the admonition, "Don't be another Avatus Stone." Stone was a black football player at the University in 1950 and 1951 whose fondness for white girls, flashy cars, and partying, caused a scandal on campus, particularly in the eyes of administrators and alumni. Some believe that Jim Brown's later criticism of Syracuse for what he regarded as poor treatment stemmed from resentment at this censorious attitude. As Mackey related, "We never felt the same way Jim did about Syracuse. He had a difficult time. We were there during the golden era. Our experiences were more pleasant."

Ernie was aware that he was constantly being looked at critically from both sides and that some may have wanted him to fail. He was protective of his image. He didn't participate in some of his teammates' high jinxs, not because he didn't enjoy rowdy good fun, but because he felt he shouldn't.

John Mackey recalled one such incident which also demonstrated the inconsistency of segregation. "I decided to integrate this restaurant in Syracuse with the help of some of my white 'Sammy' fraternity brothers. Ernie decided not to participate, but did encourage us. I got a turban and pretended to be an African prince. We were served with no problem. Ernie enjoyed that story better than anyone."

The two did get arrested once. "We were washing Ernie's car in Thornden Park one Sunday and this cop arrested us. It was for something stupid like knocking a leaf off a tree. We called Ben [Schwartzwalder] and he got us out. We never heard about it again. The cop's the one who got in trouble."

In addition to the social pressures, Ernie also had to overcome tremendous pressure generated by the expectations held for him as a star athlete. Was he good enough? Mackey stated, "Blacks weren't recruited to sit on the bench. We were expected to start." As his college career indicates he had no problem fulfilling his athletic potential. The difficult pressure came from coping with the image of Jim Brown, Syracuse's immortal football All-American. A student of the time said, "Jim Brown was held in awe at Syracuse." From the moment Ernie arrived on campus, he was the "next Jim Brown." Although Ernie played down the inevitable comparisons, they continued throughout his career.

Before he had ever played a single game for Syracuse, Ernie was asked by reporters about his and Brown's abilities.

> I wish they wouldn't compare us. Naturally I'd like to be an All-American and right now I'm hoping and praying I'll be able to go on like Jim Brown and play professional football. But after all, I'm just getting out of high school and I've still got to prove myself.

Later in his career as he progressed, the comparison question became more frequent. Ernie still attempted to remain aloof from the topic. "Guys like Jim Brown come once in a million years. I just want to play like Ernie Davis."

In a *Sport* Magazine article in fall 1963, Jim Brown wrote of the pressure on Ernie at Syracuse:

> The big thing that worried him about going there was me. I had broken football records there, became an All-American. My shadow fell on Ernie. Would he be as good as Jim Brown?

> Would he be better than Jim Brown? Did he want to be another
> Jim Brown? These were the questions immediately asked by
> the sportswriters. By saying the wrong things, he could have
> put both of us in a funny spot. He handled the delicate situa-
> tion perfectly. He simply said he respected my ability but he
> wanted to make it on his own, in his own way. To me, that is the
> mark of a great athlete and I developed the deepest respect for
> him.

At most universities with national athletic programs,
there are ambivalent feelings among the students concerning an athletes' academic abilities. Syracuse was no excep-
tion. Athletes had to prove themselves in the classroom as
well as on the athletic field. They had to live down an oft-
quoted line attributed to a legendary player, "I came here
to carry the ball, not the book." Unlike the typical jock,
however, Ernie was serious about his studies. He had
gained a respect for education from his grandparents, who
like many of their generation, believed that education
would lead to social and economic success. Mackey said,
"Ernie felt pressure to get a degree. Being an All-American
didn't matter as much as getting a degree. He couldn't go
home without it." Aware of the comparative shortness of a
professional football career, Ernie majored in business,
which he felt would help him in the job market after he
retired from football. In the classroom, Ernie was popular
with his professors and classmates. He often took his text-
books on football roadtrips and never had serious academic problems. One former student recalled, "Ernie
helped the image of athletes academically." The respect
Ernie had for education was shown in a touching way at his
commencement exercises in Archbold Stadium in June
1962. Ernie was one of two senior class marshalls who led
the graduation parade. He was selected as the graduating
senior who had contributed the most to the university,
scholastically and athletically. Wearing his ROTC uniform,
Ernie conducted the graduates to their positions on the
field and escorted the recipients of graduate degrees to the
platform to accept their honors.

University Chancellor William P. Tolley, conferring an

honorary degree on U.S. Judge Henry F. Friendly of Elmira, interrupted his reading of the degree to comment in reference to Elmira—"A town made famous by a marshall here who is graduating this morning." The audience understood and applauded. Finally Ernie and eight other class leaders were called to the platform to receive their diplomas from the Chancellor. The applause of the crowd was a fitting end to Ernie Davis' career in Archbold Stadium.

To commemorate this important occasion and to show his appreciation to those who had helped him attain it, Ernie had plaques made for them. His mother recalled, "He was always grateful for whatever anybody did for him."

The inscription reads:

This Scroll Is Presented To

Upon My Graduation From
Syracuse University
In Appreciation For Your Devotion
Confidence, Understanding
And Guidance In Helping Me
To Achieve This Important Plateau
In My Life
June 1962
(signed) Ernie Davis

The pride of accomplishment Ernie felt on graduation from college was well earned. He had proven himself socially, athletically and academically under some trying circumstances. His success is vividly recalled by those who knew him. Dr. Michael O. Sawyer summed up his appreciation of Ernie: "He was a total gentleman. He had presence. He was quiet and yet I don't think he was ever anywhere that people were not aware that he was there. He was very special." Syracuse University football coach Ben Schwartzwalder said, "It was his presence. He was turned on from the minute he woke till he went to bed. He sparkled."

Ernie's greatest achievements during college were on the

athletic field. As a sophomore he led Syracuse to the number one ranking in the country, as a junior he made All-American, and as a senior he won the Heisman Trophy. He accepted his success with a modesty that is uncommon among today's athletes. As in other aspects of his life, his achievements were the result not only of innate ability, but also of a tireless striving for self-improvement.

Mackey said: "Ernie was well liked by teammates because he wasn't arrogant and he performed. As long as you perform, what can they say? He did get in a fight with a teammate whose name I can't remember. It was behind Watson Dorm. I don't remember what it was about but they became friendly afterwards."

High school and college teammate Bill Fitzgerald summarized Davis' football skills, "Ernie was a great defensive player. He was a hard-nosed tackler. As a runner he could run over you or step around you. He had great speed but it didn't look like he was running fast. However, as somebody said, 'No one ever catches him.' His mind was always in the game. He knew he had a job to do, and he did it."

Syracuse University enjoyed its greatest football success during Ernie's career. The team's record was 24-5 plus two bowl victories. As a result of that success, there were criticisms and allegations against the program. The most serious was that cash payments were made to players based on their performance.

The allegation received national publicity when Dave Meggyesy, a former Syracuse lineman 1960-62 and a seven year veteran linebacker for the St. Louis Cardinals, wrote a book, *Out of Their League,* which was critical of what he referred to as the "dehumanizing" aspects of football. In the book he alleged Syracuse football players were given weekly pay envelopes.

In 1982 Ron Luciano, an All-American football player at Syracuse University in 1958, a former pro football player, an American League baseball umpire for 12 years, and a baseball broadcaster for NBC, wrote a best-selling book, *The Umpire Strikes Back.* He confirmed the substance of Meggyesy's charge by describing his "on-campus jobs" as bench watcher and laundry-room sweeper for which he was paid.

Not surprisingly no one wished to speak on the record about this topic. There can be little doubt that some alumni did give players cash and clothing. As the star of the team, Ernie must have participated. However, no one agreed with Meggyesy that payoffs were as systematic as he alleges or that coaches were involved. One person said, "The coaches probably knew about it but they certainly didn't participate the way Meggyesy suggested." There was agreement that, "things were done that way in those days." The practice stopped, they say, in the early sixties.

Ernie's success was forged in part by an unusual desire to practice. "He loved to practice, which is rare," said Schwartzwalder. "It's like a guy who loves to shovel dirt." A firm believer in conditioning he always kept himself in top physical shape. He never let himself go even during the off season.

Mackey recalled, "He was an excellent practice player. He lapped everyone. He went all out. Everyone knew that was his way. Many players are afraid of "leaving it" on the practice field and having nothing left for the game. Ernie had so much energy that was never a concern for him."

He enjoyed practicing so much that he wouldn't quit when the formal practice ended. If the fourth string quarterback wanted to practice passing, Ernie would stay and run pass routes for him. If no one else was around, Ernie would practice kicking or starts. He'd throw passes to one of the team managers. Schwartzwalder recalled, "The only problem you ever had with him was trying to get him off the football field. The average kid can't wait to get in the barn. Ernie'd say, 'Coach, I need the work.' "

The only one to complain about his enthusiasm for practice was the groundskeeper who wanted to turn out the lights and go home. The groundskeeper would complain to the coach, "Ben, that kid is nuts." Schwartzwalder explained, "Ernie would sweet talk him. 'Just give me another five minutes,' he'd say. The five would drag into 20 every night. Finally I told the groundskeeper, 'Just turn the lights off and he'll take the hint. We'll retrieve the ball in the morning.' "

Ernie's enthusiasm on the practice field was a morale booster for his teammates. During a scrimmage, for example, he would break tackles on a long gain, despite blocks being missed. Instead of criticizing the lack of blocking, he would encourage everyone, "Great blocking. Way to go." Schwartzwalder would say, "Ernie, you're going to be elected President of the United States someday. You'll be a great politician. You lie as well as any of them. These guys didn't block a lick, and here you're telling them how great they are. How am I going to coach these guys with you talking like that?"

Ernie set high levels of performance and was extremely self-critical. After a game in which he scored twice and rushed for over 100 yards, Ernie was disappointed. "I didn't have it," he said. "I messed up that lateral in the second quarter." That was the play he remembered on a day any player would have loved. In the October 1960 issue of *Boy's Life* magazine he described why he stayed in top shape, "If I'm in better condition than the other fellow, I have a real advantage on him. I have that crucial extra step or a quicker start, or more boom."

There was a practical motive for his penchant for being in top physical condition and practicing constantly. Chuck Davis remembered asking him what it felt like on a long touchdown run with 50,000 fans cheering for him? "Ernie responded, 'I don't hear the crowd. I think about how embarrassing it would be to be caught from behind. I think about that in practice too, when I don't feel like running laps or wind sprints. It's important what you do in practice because it pays off in the game.'"

Coach Schwartzwalder's fondest memories are of Ernie's enthusiasm. His appraisal of him was remarkably similar to those given by high school coaches Marty Harrigan and Jim Flynn. The college coach said, "Ernie led by enthusiasm and by example. His enthusiasm rubbed off on the rest. It couldn't help but rub off on them. It rubbed off on the coaching staff."

The Syracuse coaching staff had been so impressed with Ernie's high school career that he was the starting halfback the moment he arrived on campus. "If that was the toughest decision a coach had to make," said a laughing Schwartzwalder, "the student body could have made that decision." Ernie, the only black player, led the 1958 freshmen team to its first undefeated season in Syracuse history. Against the Cortland jayvees he scored 32 points. Frosh coach Les Dye said of Ernie's 63-yard touchdown run against Colgate, "a thing of beauty which had to be seen because it can't be described". His freshman success, however, was only a harbinger of the three varsity years to follow.

As great as everyone expected Ernie to be, nobody at Syracuse anticipated the 1959 football season. The Orangemen became the national champions and winners of the Cotton Bowl. The prognosis for the season depended upon how well the veterans from the previous year's team, which lost 21-6 to Oklahoma in the Orange Bowl, would blend with the untested sophomores, particularly in the backfield. Because of uncertainty on this score, Syracuse was voted only a contender in the East along with Penn State and Navy in preseason forecasts.

Right halfback, Ger Schwedes, a senior and fullback, Art Baker, a junior, were experienced veterans who would become pros. Ernie was the left halfback and fellow sophomores Dave Sarette and Dick Easterly were the quarterbacks. By season's end, the performances of all three rookies contributed heavily to the team's success. For the first of three seasons each, Ernie and Sarette led the Orangemen in rushing and passing respectively. Ernie gained 686 yards on 98 carries for a 7-yard average per rush and was also the team's second leading scorer with ten touchdowns.

The front line was one of the finest in college history and was nicknamed "The Sizeable Seven" because they averaged 6'3" and 216 pounds per man, unusually large for that era. Five of the seven became professionals, Al Bemiller, Roger Davis, Bruce Tarbox, Bob Yates, and Maury Youmans. The second team line included three future pros, John Brown, Tom Gilburg and Gene Grabosky.

The 1959 team still holds 21 all-time Syracuse records, eleven on defense and ten on offense. With the powerful lines, the Orangemen excelled at rushing defense, allowing .6 of a yard per attempt. Four opponents, Holy Cross, Pittsburgh, Boston University, and UCLA, lost more yards rushing than they gained.

Offensively, Syracuse lived up to its reputation as a rushing team but they also set two important passing standards, completing 58.1% of their attempts and connecting on 21 touchdown passes. On the ground they averaged 313.6 yards per game for a 5.5 yard average per carry.

For the season, the Orangemen led the nation in total offense, total defense and 16 other statistical categories. The success and dominance of the team was not anticipated by the head coach:

> We knew we were going to be a good football team. But to win all the games—has to be beyond your expectations. It's dependent on so many things. That year, particularly, we were fortunate we never had an injury until the Cotton Bowl game. That's a prominent part of the battle—not to have a key person hurt.

It's important to note that two rule changes have occurred in college football since Ernie played, which directly affects comparisons of individual or team performances with todays athletes. Unlike today, freshmen were not eligible to play varsity sports. More importantly, one-platoon football was the system then, rather than the two-platoon system of today.

Under the one-platoon system, a player performed both offensively and defensively, while his unit was on the field. Syracuse played the first unit approximately five minutes and then substituted the entire second unit of eleven men. Moreover, there were no special teams for kicking situations. While on the field, a player was involved in all the kicking plays.

The two-platoon system of today calls for exchanging offensive and defensive units according to ball possession. Very few, if any, of the first string players play on the special teams. A running back from the Davis and Jim Brown era played offense, defense, and special teams, while later runners like O. J. Simpson or Tony Dorsett played only offense. This difference makes it difficult to compare players of the one-platoon era with players of the two-platoon era, at least in terms of statistical criteria, such as rushing yardage totals.

Coach Schwartzwalder still feels one-platoon football should not have been replaced. "The two-platoon system," said Schwatzwalder, "took something big away from the game of football and made it strictly a numbers game. Football became too specialized. It took something away from the kids and prevented them from developing as all-around athletes. Whatever they couldn't do, they had to work on. They couldn't become prima donnas. Two-platoon football hurt team spirit and togetherness. Today the kids don't even know each other because they practice separately."

Ernie realized that his greatest weakness was playing defense. "In high school, they don't neglect defensive ball," he said, "but at Syracuse, it's a deadly serious business." Having been primarily a pass rusher as a defensive end in high school and strictly a defensive back in college, Ernie was forced to make adjustments in his defensive play, particularly in passing situations. The technique he practiced included watching the quarterback's eyes and turning the receiver inside. "If I turn him inside, our secondary can gang up on him," he stated. The adjustment must not have been too difficult, because Schwartzwalder, a stickler for defense, said, "Ernie was a good defensive player. He liked to hit people. He played defense well."

Throughout his career on game days, Ernie would begin to get nervous when he got his ankles taped in the morning, and it would last through warmups to the kickoff.

> One way or the other, almost everyone feels the pressure. In my own case, I get a painful tightness down in my stomach and I don't want to talk to anyone. The kickoff comes as a sense of enormous relief to me. All of a sudden I feel my whole body loosen and relax. Then I'm myself again.

Ernie began his varsity career on an unusually warm sunny day in front of 20,000 fans at Archbold Stadium. The opponent, Kansas, was led by such future pro stars as quarterback John Hadl and halfback Curtis McClinton. Behind a powerful ground attack, the Orangemen prevailed 35-21. After the victory Coach Schwartzwalder said, "Our offense was ragged but we played some good football between errors. Ernie Davis did okay for his first game, too. I still think he's going to be a great football player."

Syracuse continued to roll against the Maryland Terrapins in the second game of the season, winning 29-0 in what *The New York Times* writer Lincoln Werden described as, "one of Syracuse's greatest modern football performances." The Orange defense recorded the first of five shutouts and limited the visitors to 29 yards total offense, which was Maryland's lowest output since they began intercollegiate football in 1882. The Terrapins' offense employed the then novel "I" formation of Coach Tom Nugent which despite the drubbing is still used today in a modified form. At that time the formation had three backs lined up directly behind the quarterback whereas today there are only two. Ernie led the Syracuse offense by gaining a game high 77 yards and scoring a touchdown on a 28-yard run.

The first "big game" of the season took place the following week in a driving rainstorm at the 13th Oyster Bowl in Norfolk, Virginia against the Naval Academy. All-American and future Heisman Trophy winner Joe Bellino led the Midshipmen into a game, the outcome of which would have a significant effect on voting for the Lambert Trophy, the award symbolic of eastern college supremacy. Syracuse was never threatened enroute to a 32-6 victory in the first game ever played between the two teams.

The Orangemen hosted the Crusaders of Holy Cross the next week seeking revenge. The visitors had earned one point victories in each of the previous two years, the second one being Syracuse's only loss of the 1958 regular season. The hosts broke the game open in the first five

As an EFA freshman basketball player with wrist still bandaged from football injury (Courtesy Al Mallette)

One of the earliest pictures of Ernie (on left); Elmira Small-Fry League, 1952 (Courtesy Al Mallette)

Relaxing at Archbold Stadium as Syracuse freshman in 1958 (Courtesy Chuck Davis)

The 1959 undefeated National Championship team and coaching staff
(Courtesy SU Sports Information)

Delivering Christmas mail during junior year (Courtesy Al
Mallette)

At practice with (left to right) Don King, Pete Brokaw and Dick Easterly (Courtesy SU Sports Information)

Cutting behind block of #82 All-American end, Fred Mautino (Courtesy Chuck Davis)

Ernie Davis, 1960 (Courtesy SU Sports Information)

Preparing to meet defender (Courtesy Chuck Davis)

Demonstrating his defensive ability, Ernie knocks down a pass (Courtesy Chuck Davis)

Varsity basketball coach, Marc Guley with football- basketball players (left to right) Ernie Davis, John Mackey and Don King (Courtesy SU Sports Information)

Basketball publicity photo listing Ernie as 6'2" jr. (Courtesy SU Sports Information)

minutes of the second quarter by scoring three touch-downs—one by Ernie on a 40-yard run—enroute to a 42-6 triumph.

The next two weeks produced consecutive shutouts, 44-0 over West Virginia and 35-0 over the University of Pittsburgh. Ernie played the most spectacular game of his career against West Virginia as he rushed for 141 yards on only nine carries. His 15.7 yards per carry average is still the Syracuse one-game individual record. He scored touchdowns on runs of 29 and 57 yards. The undefeated Orangemen, 6-0, traveled to Penn State to meet the undefeated Nittany Lions, 7-0, with the Lambert Trophy, a major bowl bid, and a national championship possible for the winner. The hosts were led by All-American senior quarterback Richie Lucas and speedy sophomore halfback Roger Kochman. Recalled Schwartzwalder, "The hardest hitting game we played was always the Penn State game, and it was usually the cleanest. When the game is really important and the other team is a skillful team, it will be a clean ball game."

The Orangemen dominated the first three quarters as they scored three touchdowns including a short run by Ernie to take a 20-6 lead. The Nittany Lions staged a fourth quarter rally and moved to within two points, 20-18. The game and the season were on the line. A ball-control drive was needed to keep the Nittany Lions at bay. Syracuse received the kickoff with 5:25 minutes remaining against the aroused Penn State team, supported by thunderous fan encouragement. With their big offensive linemen controlling the line of scrimmange, the Orangemen drove 60 yards and ran the clock out to preserve their undefeated season. With the victory, the Orangemen rose to the top of the wire service football polls for the first time in their history.

Building on the momentum of the Penn State victory, the number-one ranked Orangemen rolled through the final three games of the season. They shutout Colgate 71-0 and Boston University 46-0. After the Colgate victory, the Orangemen accepted a bid to the Cotton Bowl, their third major bowl bid in four years.

For the final game of the season, Syracuse traveled to Los Angeles and easily defeated the UCLA Bruins 36-8. *Los Angeles Examiner* reporter Morton Moss' story of the game, included in the annual anthology *Best Sports Stories*, provides an impressive verbal snapshot of the 1959 Syracuse team at the height of its power. The following is the first 11 paragraphs of the report.

> Syracuse, the beast from the East, ran amok yesterday at the Coliseum, crunching the merely human Bruins of UCLA, 36-8, in its bloody jaws.
>
> Anybody among the 46,436 witnesses of the catastrophe who doubted the Orange's right to No. 1 national rating was more than convinced by the awesomely powerful deportment of coach Ben Schwartzwalder's huge creatures. UCLA simply isn't on the same level of efficiency as Syracuse which moved with consummate ease to a perfect season of 10 victories, the first unbeaten Orange season in 72 years.
>
> Probably decisive was the tremendous line strength exerted by Syracuse, with such mighty men as guard Roger Davis and tackle Bob Yates brilliantly effective.
>
> The Orange corps of backs was well served by this line. Right halfback Ger Schwedes and Dick Easterly, the quarterback of the allegedly second unit, split the major offensive honors during Syracuse's mop-up of five touchdowns, three of them in the first half.
>
> Easterly, traveling without difficulty in an easterly or westerly direction, hurled to left halfback Mark Weber for two TD's and collected a third himself through a nudge at center. Dick, a sophomore, celebrated with five completions on as many tries.
>
> Schwedes, pulsating dynamism, tore off a 23-yard TD blast inside left end and preceded it with jaunt of 30 yards. He might have traveled the distance if he hadn't tripped over a blocker. He paced the monster Syracuse attack that compiled 460 net yards, 354 along the earth and 106 aerially. Ger the Gorgeous averaged 11 per jolt and 99 in all. He also received a TD pass from Dave Sarette.
>
> For a while there, during the third period, the cartwheeling on the field threatened to resemble a combat between equals. UCLA appeared to have solved the Syracuse land assault and was beginning to behave like a menace itself.
>
> But the exhausted Bruins couldn't absorb the Syracuse

pounding in the fourth quarter, and the Orange hustled across two more TD's. The final one followed an interception the way their initial score of the bash did.

Syracuse biceps were manifested in the Orange's approach to its touchdowns. Every one resulted from a good bag yardage. Among the hammering advances were marches of 81, 72 and 69 yards.

The Orange employed a basic T with an unbalanced line. But Schwartzwalder uses power blocking more on the order of the single wing which is UCLA's pattern.

The season ended with Syracuse earning its first national championship. The only undefeated major college team for the year, the Orangemen established still existing school records of 390 points and 56 touchdowns. The defense yielded only 59 points. Some associated with the team felt it did not receive the respect it deserved. Many believed Syracuse's dream season would not be complete without a victory in the Cotton Bowl. The bookmakers favored them by two touchdowns. The Orangemen were determined to prove they deserved their ranking and record.

Since the game would be played in the deep South, black players felt some concern about possible racial problems and expressed their worries to Coach Schwartzwalder. The previous season, while practicing in North Carolina for the Orange Bowl, the team had a party to which only white coeds from nearby colleges attended. This had made the black players feel uncomfortable, but Schwartzwalder assured them that they had no need for concern this year.

The Orangemen practiced in Houston for a week prior to arriving in Dallas for the game. Realizing their social options were limited, the black teammates rented a car so that they could visit black neighborhoods. One evening they returned after curfew and were caught. Ernie assumed responsibility, although it was not his fault. The initial reaction of the coach was to withdraw car privileges. Ernie interceded with the coach and promised not to violate the curfew. The coach relented, and the car was returned. There were no more curfew problems for the remainder of the trip.

When the Orangemen arrived in Dallas for the game, they stayed on the outskirts of the city so that black and white players could stay in the same hotel. They were determined not to repeat the experience of four years earlier—the year Jim Brown led them to the Cotton Bowl—when the entire squad had rooms on the first floor because blacks were prohibited from using the elevators.

Four days before the game, Ernie pulled a hamstring muscle while practicing place-kicks. The coach recalled, "He begged me a couple of days before the game to let him practice extra points. I said all right, but hit them easy. That son-of-a-gun not only practiced extra points, but also kickoffs. He pulled a hamstring muscle."

It was doubtful right up until game time whether Ernie could play. Schwartzwalder remembered:

> Julie Reichel, the trainer, went all over Dallas looking for rubber pants to hold the leg tight. Just before we went on the field, the doctor finally said okay. I didn't know how good he was going to be. You couldn't trust him. In warmups I said, "Ernie, don't you dare go over half speed. Just get loosened up." In tough games Ernie always came through.

In a memorable clutch performance, Ernie led the Orangemen to their first bowl victory, 23-14. Before leaving the game late in the fourth quarter with leg cramps, Ernie scored two touchdowns, including a then bowl record pass play, scored twice on two-point conversions, and intercepted a pass that led to Syracuse's final touchdown.

Not surprisingly he was voted the game's Most Valuable Player, but he did not receive the award in the planned formal ceremony. This was supposed to have taken place at a banquet after the game. But when Cotton Bowl officials explained that only white players could attend and that Ernie would be allowed only to receive the award but not to eat, the Syracuse team declined to attend.

Syracuse began auspiciously and maintained the lead throughout the game. Texas rallied in the second half, behind a surprisingly strong ground attack. For the game, the Longhorns outgained the vaunted Orangemen in rushing 145 to 133. On Syracuse's third play from scrimmage, halfback Ger Schwedes hit Ernie with an option pass that culminated in a bowl record 87-yard touchdown. Ironically, the play broke the record of 79 yards set the year before by Oklahoma against Syracuse in the Orange Bowl.

Schwartzwalder recalled the play vividly:

> It was a reverse pass by Schwedes. Ernie was supposed to go out in the flat. He saw the halfback and safety double up on our end, leaving the middle wide open. Ernie cut into the middle and Schwedes picked him up. He's 20 yards in the open. No one is near him. I'm running down the sidelines. It's a wonder they didn't penalize me because I got beyond the 35 yard line. You can't go beyond those 35's. I'm screaming, "Slow down. Slow down. Please don't pull it."

The nationally televised game was marred by fighting, including a bench clearing brawl prior to halftime. Both *Life* magazine and *The Today Show* on television focussed on the fighting in their coverage of the game. The *Life* article editorialized:

> As the game moved back and forth on the field and the normal tensions of the players were increased by the bone-crunching fury of the play, an ugly undercurrent of racial bitterness began to spread—with shocking results. At first in the game the Syracuse players out-did themselves in showing what good sports they were, helping blocked Texans off the ground and slapping their rumps for friendly good measure. But this was short-lived.

Just before halftime, Syracuse quarterback Dick Easterly passed 41 yards to end Ken Ericson for an apparent touchdown. The play was nulified, however, by a holding penalty. At that point the fighting began, and both benches emptied onto the field. Schwartzwalder ran onto the field to protest the call and was penalized. After several minutes, order was restored.

In the locker room after the game, Syracuse linemen Al Gerlick and Al Bemiller maintained that the halftime fight was the result of a racial slur against teammate John Brown by a Texas player. Longhorn guard Babe Dreymala said that Brown picked up Texas tackle Larry Stephens as if to slam him to the ground. According to Dreymala, when he intervened, the fighting began.

The *Life* article subtitled "Climax of Bitterness" gave this account: "To goad him off balance," Brown claimed, "Stephens kept calling him a 'big black dirty nigger.' Finally Brown warned him not to call him that again. When Stephens did, Brown swung. Afterward, Stephens apologized to Brown. But Brown had already forgiven him. 'That Texas boy was just excited,' he said. 'Let's forget it.' Brown declined to comment on the incident when questioned about it 20 years later saying simply, "It was a long time ago."

The Today Show on NBC wanted Ernie to appear, which he agreed to do with the stipulation that no questions would be asked about the fighting. Ernie felt that with feelings still so high on both sides, it would be inappropriate to discuss it at that time. The show's officials agreed, but when Ernie appeared, he was asked the questions anyway. Ernie wasn't upset by the bad faith of the producers, but he was sorry that his answers weren't better prepared. He said, "I hadn't been able to give enough thought to the problem. I never faced this kind of prejudice before."

In the fall of 1960, such outstanding linemen and future pros as John Mackey, Dave Meggyesy and Walt Sweeney, joined the varsity and Syracuse remained a potent rushing team. It was to be Ernie's best season statistically. He became the third leading rusher in the nation with 877 yards and a still-standing Syracuse record of 7.8 yards per carry average. He rushed for over 100 yards in six of the nine games with a season's high of 130 versus Miami. At season's end, he was named All-American. Ernie, however, was disappointed because the team finished with a 7-2 record and no bowl bid.

Before the season started, Ernie and teammate Fred Mautino, an end, were chosen as All-Americans by *Playboy*. That was the first time, in what is now an annual event, that the players were flown to the magazine's headquaters in Chicago for the weekend and photographed together. Ernie was the only black player on a team that included such future professional stars as Bob Lilly of Texas Christian, E.J. Holub of Texas Tech, Bill Brown of Illinois and Marlin MeKeever of USC.

When interviewed, *Playboy* sports editor Anson Mount said:

> To pick an Ernie Davis for an All-American is not difficult. Everybody could pick Ernie Davis. He was the greatest running back who ever lived up to that time. He had agility and speed, which makes a runner great today. Prior to him with the exception of Ernie Nevers, you had defensive tackles carrying the ball who just overpowered everybody with brute force.

Playboy picked the Orangemen to finish second in the country and first in the East with an 8-1 record. Mount wrote:

> In the East, Syracuse is loaded again. Coach Ben Schwartzwalder has been shedding tears for some departed linemen, but he isn't eliciting any sympathy from us. The Orange is still fat and healthy, and the boys from Syracuse have a backfield unequaled anywhere in the country. Speedy halfback Ernie Davis and end Fred Mautino are among the best in college football.

The season began well for Ernie. On the first play from scrimmage in the season's opener against Boston University at Archbold Stadium, he ran 80 yards for a touchdown off the right side on the famed Syracuse scissors play. Always modest, Ernie said after the game, "I didn't do it by myself, you know. Those blockers wiped everyone out. . . A little kid could have run that one."

The team won its first five for a three-year regular season winning streak of 22, and was ranked third in the country. Syracuse survived a close call in the fourth game against visiting Penn State. They built a 21-7 lead on an 18-yard run by Davis, a 62-yard interception return by Mark Weber, and a touchdown run by Don King. Nittany Lion quarterback Galen Hall rallied his team to eight fourth quarter points and had them on the Syracuse four yard line as time expired.

After shutting out West Virginia 45-0 in the fifth game, the host Orangemen were heavily favored over a 2-2-1

University of Pittsburgh team. An all-time record Archbold Stadium crowd of 41,872 watched in disbelief as the
Panthers behind Jim Traficant, Mike Ditka, and Fred Cox,
upset Syracuse 10-0.

It was the Orangemen's first regular season loss after 22
straight victories dating from the third game of the 1958
season; although they had lost 21-6 to Oklahoma in the
Orange Bowl on New Year's Day 1959. Since then they had
the longest winning streak in college football, 16 games.
The Orangemen were thwarted by a Pitt defense that
forced six turnovers and held them to only 188 yards total
offense. For Ernie who had a couple of fumbles it was his
first loss since high school.

The following story by reporter Bill Clark of the *Syracuse
Herald American* was selected as the best-news feature of the
year in the annual book, *Best Sports Stories.*

> This is the way the longest winning streak in college football
> came to an end: Not with a bang! Not with a whimper! But in
> complete silence.
>
> On the Syracuse bench, you could feel the Orange's 16-game
> streak dying from the first quarter on. It was a slow death—a
> lingering, brutal, frustrating thing that tore emotion out of the
> Orangemen.
>
> The warm sun of a perfect October Saturday shone directly
> into their eyes as the Orange alternates and bench-bound
> reserves knelt in front of their benches. It made them squint as
> they anxiously followed every play.
>
> Earlier cries of encouragement to the players on the field
> were many: "Hit them guys! That's a baby—way to hit!" Come
> on you guys, let's go!" "Get tough, gang!"
>
> Only the passage of time dulled the spirited yells from the
> bench. Expressionless faces alternately glanced at the action on
> the field and the scoreboard clock as the game lumbered into
> its final minutes.
>
> Pitt was still moving relentlessly forward, running out the
> clock and all of Syracuse's hopes. Despite the warm sun, the
> chill of approaching defeat made Ben Schwartzwalder put on
> his warmup jacket. He stood silently in front of the bench,
> arms on hips, sternly watching and waiting for what was now
> inevitable.
>
> To one kneeling there, the only feeling was the soggy cold of

the soft, wet turf seeping through the pants legs about the knees.

The eyes could see the blue and gold clad Panthers and the Orange and White Syracusans ramming into each other with a little less authority than they had earlier.

The ears heard the single hand-clap of the Pitt players as they left their huddle. There was the rhythmic guttural "uh, uh, uh" of the Pitt quarterback as he called his signals. And thud, thud, thud, of hard running feet. The official's whistle as he came running up to announce the death of another play. The PA system called off each advance, who made it, and who stopped it. A trumpeter in the Pitt band across the way kept blowing "charge."

Finally, it was over. Then came the long walk across the field. For many of the Orangemen it was their first walk off a college gridiron in defeat. Helmets in hand, they walked directly into the still high-on-the-sky sun. Their shadows trailed off behind them at each step.

Into the field stand area they walked. The stands formed a tunnel of staring humanity which led into the real tunnel leading on to the locker rooms.

The stares of the spectators were cruel. Most of the Syracuse players kept their heads bowed to avoid the looks. The players said nothing. Some spectators who had quickly forgotten the long string of 16 wins yelled abuse like "Ya bums, you're no good, ya deserved to lose." One of these loyal fans figured his $4.50 admission charge entitled him to throw his program down on the players in rage.

Inside the locker room, the silence of the players continued. No one banged down a helmet, no one threw off his jersey in rage, no one kicked a locker. In many places, tears welled in the corners of eyes. But none were shed. The Orange lost like men.

The Hillmen took defeat as devoid of outward signs of emotion as they had taken many of their most glorious victories sans outward signs of elation. Inwardly, though, the boys were tearing their hearts out with rage.

This inward tension exploded alongside the bench late in the ball game. A loud mouth stood there calling Ben Schwartzwalder some awful names. Ben did nothing about the name caller. Gary Fallon and some other reserves did: they leaped upon him and beat the daylights out of him.

In the dressing room, the still mute players shed their equipment. Not one word was spoken until their head coach came and asked:

"May I have your attention, please? Don't let this throw you. We have three more games to play—you can go a long way down or a long way up. Knowing you, I believe you will come back from this defeat against Army next week."

The players almost cheered but they had already shown out beside the bench what they think of Benny.

The silence returned, broken only by the increasing splash of water from the shower room as the players washed away the sweat and grime of play. One of the showers splashed on long after all the players had departed the locker room.

Upstairs, Ben, and aides Rocky Pirro, Roy Simmons, Bill Bell and Ted Dailey sat quietly on benches. The bright sun splashed through an open window. If the Orange had lost to a lesser team than Pitt, the beautiful day would have been a terrible mocker.

But as Ben said: "Pitt beat us. It was no fluke. They were the best team out there today. They outplayed us and we have no alibis."

Simmons, who had scouted Pitt, mused "we just gave them the ball too many times. Pitt played a normal game for them. But previously this year, they didn't get the opportunities they got today. And they didn't pass today as much as usual, of course, they didn't have to."

Bell thought "our kids may have tried too hard. They were not loose on offense the way you must be."

As for outstanding players on both sides, Ben said "We saw too much of that (Mike) Ditka. Pete Brokaw was our best back—he's a souped-up kid. Freddie Mautino did all right for us."

Simmons praised Pitt fullback Jim Cunningham. "He had a good day offensively and defensively. I thought Tom Gilburg played a fine game in our line."

Ben commented on Ernie Davis' fumbles. "Ernie said he got hit before he got the ball—we just weren't blocking for our backs."

Ben thought the Orange defensive play was all right. "I figured we would need three touchdowns to win. As it turned out, we could have won with two. We've got to keep our defense where it is and pick up our offense."

Ben thought his kids' reaction to defeat was okay. "They acted civilized and took it like gentlemen."

"Next week is Army—and a new season. We've got to forget about Pitt until next year. Losing is always hard, but if somebody had to beat us—and we knew somebody did—I don't object to Pitt being the ones to do it."

"Well, I might as well take a shower," Ben tried to joke, "There's no use staying dirty."

Ben was hurt to the core, but like his players wasn't showing it any more than he could help.

Despite Coach Schwartzwalder's efforts to get the players up for the Army game the following week, Syracuse lost 9–6 to the Cadets in Yankee Stadium. For the game, Schwartzwalder changed the offense, therefore, Ernie did not carry the ball very often. He was used mostly as a decoy, which prompted an army colonel in the press box to remark, "If Syracuse doesn't want to run Davis, give him to us. We'll run him into All-American." By season's end, Ernie made All-American and Schwartzwalder said, "He's the best back in the country."

The team bounced back to win its final two games. In the finale they beat Miami of Florida 21–14 at the Orange Bowl. The team stayed in a Miami Beach Hotel. Mackey recalled, "It was so segregated it didn't even have black maids. We decided to integrate the pool. When we got in, all the whites except for our teammates, got out. Since Ernie and I couldn't swim we just sat on the edge and put our feet in the water. Finally a white kid jumped in, then a few more, and the pool was integrated."

At the Orange Bowl the seating was segregated with black ticket holders permitted to sit only in the end zone seats. The black players led by Art Baker thought about not playing in protest but in the end decided to play.

In February, with the basketball team struggling through a dismal 2–12 season, Ernie, John Mackey, and fellow football player Don King joined the team at Coach Marc Guley's request. Coach Schwartzwalder encouraged participation in other sports. "I was all for them playing everything, just not during football season," he recalled. "We had basketball, baseball, lacrosse, wrestling and track performers. We told them when they were recruited they could do more than one. Anything that gives you a lift— that's wholesome and good."

Mackey maintains that Ernie's first athletic love was basketball. "He had great moves," said Mackey, "and he was a good shooter". I think the reason he concentrated on football was because he felt he had a better chance in football than in basketball to make the pros. He probably wasn't a good enough ball handler to be a pro guard or big enough to be a pro forward."

Coach Guley told a reporter at the time, "The whole thing was a tremendous surprise. We had Ernie as a freshman, and he was the best we had. But with football and the Cotton Bowl, we lost him last year. I had hopes, but I never expected to see him back on the court. He's made a difference." The team won two of six including an upset at Penn State in which Ernie scored 21 points. In a game against Canisius, he had 15 points and 18 rebounds while still not in condition for basketball.

Guley marveled, "You just don't stay away from basketball like Ernie has and move back without feeling the effects. You've got to get your shooting touch back and you've got to condition different muscles. But Ernie has that terrific desire. He's simply a great athlete." Mackey said, "Ernie didn't have a difficult adjustment period switching from football to basketball." Ernie's abilities were evident to the legendary St. John's coach Joe Lapchick, "He's so aggressive I'd think he'd be inclined to foul out, yet he rebounds and . . . he's better than anything they had." Guley said wistfully, "I'd sure like to start a season with him just once."

Athletes who can perform in more than one sport on the collegiate level are rare. In the October 16, 1961 issue of *Sports Illustrated* in a feature article on Terry Baker of Oregon State, Ernie was listed with six others as noteworthy all-around athletes. Among the six were, Roman Gabriel, North Carolina State; Curtis McClinton, Kansas; and Pat Richter, Wisconsin, a three-sport star. All three went on to become professional football players, while Baker, who succeeded Ernie as the Heisman Trophy winner, had a short pro-football career.

Ernie's final football season was personally a highly rewarding one and the hallmarks included; *Sports Illustrated's*

"Back of the Week," four times weekly All-East, a consensus All-American, and the Heisman Trophy. Once again he was selected as pre-season *Playboy* All-American. He was joined on the team by another black player, Larry Ferguson of Iowa. Others chosen included, Ronnie Bull of Baylor, Gary Collins of Maryland, Roy Winston of LSU, Gabriel and Richter. He led the team in rushing for the third successive year, gaining over 100 yards three times and over 90 yards on three other occasions. He led the team in scoring with 15 touchdowns.

His final season was even more extraordinary, because of injury problems he overcame and because most opposing coaches believed that if you stopped Ernie, you stopped Syracuse. "Ernie was crippled up a bit that last year," Schwartzwalder said. "It affected him, but he played. They were all out to get acquainted with Ernie. When you run the ball that much, they are going to take a lot of shots at you."

Playboy picked Syracuse to be ninth nationally with a 9–1 record. Sports editor Mount surmised,

> The main thing wrong with Syracuse last year was that they appeared to be a little tired of winning. So they had a "bad" season by winning only seven games and losing two. But this year the Orange is on the rebound: with Ernie Davis returning at halfback (unquestionably the top college runner in the nation) and an experienced and belligerent line up front, Syracuse could be just as difficult to deal with as they were a couple of years ago when they won the National Championship. But a tougher schedule than usual will probably keep them out of the undefeated ranks.

With two close losses, the Orange's 7–3 record was a disappointment but it still earned a bowl bid.

The Orangemen opened the season on the road against Oregon State University, a team led by halfback Terry Baker. Syracuse won 19–8 but Ernie was terribly banged up, suffering two sprained ankles and a right shoulder bruise so severe he couldn't raise his arm above his head. The injuries prevented him from practicing for the following week's home opener against West Virginia. During

Ernie's two previous varsity years, he had played extremely well against the Mountaineers, and the Syracuse defense had shut them out both times. Despite their previous success, the one thing the Orangemen knew for certain was that the West Virginia game would be physical because of their big, strong, tough linemen. During the game, Ernie's ankle was twisted by the same West Virginia tackle after each of his first three carries. Ernie ignored it the first two times. On the third occasion, Ernie smiled at the culprit and said, "What's this? What's going on?" The tackle, expecting a violent response, became embarrassed and said, "Ernie, I'm sorry." That was the last time Ernie's ankle was twisted that day.

Syracuse won the game 29–14, but Ernie was held to just 34 yards rushing. Coach Schwartzwalder remembered,

80-yard touchdown run against Boston University, 1960 (Courtesy Al Mallette)

"On TV he was asked if he was bothered by his injuries. Ernie said no, he just had a bad day. He wanted no part of an alibi, not even a legitimate one."

After a heartbreaking loss to Maryland 22–21, Syracuse got back on the track with a 28–6 win over Nebraska. As a result of his performance, 120 yards rushing and two touchdowns, which established a new Syracuse career scoring record, Ernie was selected *Sports Illustrated's* "Back of the Week."

The Orangemen's three-year winning streak against Penn State ended with a 14–0 loss, but the team rebounded with two straight resounding wins at home; 34–6 over Holy Cross and 28–9 over the University of Pittsburgh. Pitt lineman Gary Kaltenback was asked by a west coast sportswriter to name the top team played by the Panthers this year, "Ernie Davis," he said.

The next week versus Colgate was Ernie's final home game at Archbold Stadium. For the first time since the season's opener, his shoulder felt good enough to throw the option pass, and he connected with his roommate John Mackey on a 74 yard touchdown. It is the fourth longest touchdown pass in Syracuse history. Ernie lead the Orangemen to a 51–8 victory over the Red Raiders. It was the last meeting, for many years, between the two schools after 62 straight games with Colgate holding the winning record 31–26–5.

Syracuse finished the season with two road games against Notre Dame and Boston College. The team's trip to South Bend, Indiana, to play Notre Dame was the first meeting between the two schools since 1914, and the game turned out to be one of the most controversial in NCAA history. Ernie was excited about the chance to play Notre Dame, because he had been a fan of Notre Dame Heisman Trophy winner Leon Hart. Moreover, he had once thought seriously about attending Notre Dame.

Knowing the Irish defense would be keying on Ernie, Coach Schwartzwalder decided to use him as a decoy, faking the ball to him and putting him in motion. Ernie wore a lineman's shoulder pads to absorb the expected heavy pounding from the Irish linemen led by Nick Buoniconti. Wherever Ernie went the Irish followed, enabling the other Syracuse runners to gain yardage. The strategy appeared to succeed as Syracuse clung to a 15–14 lead and had just intercepted a pass in the closing moments. As usual, Schwartzwalder sent in a play. He had called a running play. The messenger with visions of stardom flashing through his mind, arrived in the huddle saying, "The coach wants to win big" and gave the quarterback a pass play. As Schwartzwalder said ten years later, "I didn't want to win big. I wanted to win by one point." Notre Dame intercepted the pass but Schwartzwalder ruefully noted, "Our receiver was wide open. The pass was underthrown."

Irish sophomore quarterback Frank Budka engineered a drive to the Syracuse 39-yard line. With three seconds remaining and kicking into a strong wind, Joe Perkowski of Notre Dame attempted a 56-yard field goal. Under the conditions, Schwartzwalder didn't want a hard rush, but the excited Orangemen poured through. The kick was partially blocked. The Syracuse bench was ecstatic. Then they saw a penalty flag thrown by the head linesman. Syracuse was penalized 15 yards for roughing the holder. Given a second chance, Perkowski was successful from 41 yards for a 17–15 Notre Dame victory.

A rules controversy quickly developed over which team had possession of the ball when the roughing occurred. Replays clearly showed the ball had been kicked and blocked before Walt Sweeney of Syracuse pushed Perkowski into the holder George Sefcik. Most sports experts held that once the ball had been kicked, it was no longer in Notre Dame's possession.

Paul Menton, sports editor of the Baltimore *Evening Sun* and a 30-year college official, questioned the legality of Notre Dame's winning kick. Dr. Edward A. Geiges, secretary of the NCAA rules committee, observed that the game should have ended with the first kick. The commissioners of the Big Ten and Eastern Collegiate Athletic Conference, which supplied the officials, issued a joint statement that the second kick should not have been permitted.

A discrepancy in the rules was discovered as the controversy continued. Notre Dame supporters cited a rule, "Although a free ball, a scrimmage kick from behind A's line [Notre Dame] is treated as though in the possession of team A if the penalty for roughing the kicker is accepted." The experts on the Syracuse side of the dispute quoted a rule, "A foul during a kick, including roughing the kicker, will not extend the period as the ball is not in the kicking team's possession."

Schwartzwalder stated, "The way the rules were written at that time when the game is over, it's over. By the time our kids got back to where the holder was, the game was over by two seconds. Whatever happened after that is of no consequence. The rule was changed that winter at the coaches meeting. That was a little tardy because the game wasn't played after the coaches meeting. It was definitely a boo-boo on the part of the officials."

The controversy gained nationwide media attention. Many were reminded of the 1940 Cornell-Dartmouth game. Cornell apparently won 7–3 but two days later the referee discovered that he had permitted Cornell a fifth down on which they scored the winning touchdown. After the discovery, Cornell conceded the victory to Dartmouth. The new dispute was so well publicized that President John F. Kennedy, in a speech in New York compared the game to his own narrow electoral victory. "Many people," he said, "think my victory was like Notre Dame's over Syracuse. Like Notre Dame, I'm not going to give mine back."

Prior to the final game of the season, the Syracuse squad, in a close vote, opted for the Liberty Bowl over the Gotham City Bowl in New York City. The Liberty Bowl organizers endeavored to persuade Notre Dame to accept the other bid to replay the controversial game. The Irish refused because, at that time, Notre Dame had a policy of not participating in bowl games. It was the Orangemen's fifth bowl bid and their third in four years, however, they were still somewhat disappointed. According to Schwartz-walder, they had been promised an Orange Bowl bid if they defeated Notre Dame, which they felt they had.

In his last regular season college game, Ernie broke Jim Brown's total offense record, but it was his defensive play in the final minutes that proved decisive in Syracuse's 28–13 victory. Entering the game, Ernie needed only 15 yards to surpass Brown, and he totaled 207.

Syracuse took a 14–7 lead in the third quarter on an 18-yard touchdown pass from Dave Sarette to John Mackey. With two minutes remaining in the game Boston College scored. They attempted a two-point conversion and Ernie made the first of his outstanding defensive plays, as he kept the intended receiver away from the pass after Mackey put on a big pass rush. With a minute remaining, Ernie intercepted a pass and sprinted 63 yards down the sidelines for a touchdown to seal the victory. Syracuse fullback Gary Fallon intercepted Boston College's final pass and ran it back 25 yards for a score to provide the final victory margin.

With the conclusion of the regular season, Ernie had eclipsed ten of Jim Brown's standards. Throughout the season, as Ernie set new records, comparisons and opinions about which of the All-Americans was the best were rampant. To this day you can still get in an argument in Syracuse over who was better.

That argument will never be resolved. There is agreement that the two helped establish a winning football tradition that Jim Nance, Floyd Little and Larry Csonka continued. Brown, Davis and Little in succession wore jersey 44, making it one of the most famous numbers in college football. Even today, almost every store on Marshall Street, near the campus, sells number 44 jerseys or displays pictures of the former stars.

In his freshman year, Ernie told reporters, "I know one thing. I am not another Jim Brown. I'm not that good." One who later did not agree was *New York Herald Tribune* sports editor Stanley Woodward, who chose Ernie over Brown in the fall of 1961. While conceding Ernie played on better teams, Woodward wrote:

> Davis has abilities Brown never showed as a college player. Brown didn't block, but Davis does. Brown was not much of a pass receiver; Davis is superb. Brown could pass a little; Davis is better. Brown was a fierce stomping runner, practically all power; Davis has power but he can streak his way through a broken field and use casual blockers. Brown was a fair defensive player; Davis is a good one.

Sandy Grady of the *Philadelphia Evening Bulletin* wrote:

> Davis has much of Brown's inherent dignity, although he is more outgoing and less moody. People who watched both say Davis may lack Brown's stallion power, but at Syracuse he was the more complete performer, a quicker runner, a better thrower and catcher, a better blocker, and superb on defense. He may never reach Brown's zenith as a pro, but certainly he will sign for a rookie salary more plush than Brown ever dreamed.

A person who has steadfastly never given his opinion is coach Schwartzwalder:

> They all want me to compare Jim, Ernie, Floyd [Little], and Larry [Csonka] and you just don't do that. You'd like to have all four on the same team and then figure out who's going to play quarterback. Jim would play quarterback because he was the best passer. Then people would say you're an idiot for playing Jim Brown at quarterback.

Ernie always strived for excellence and was extremely competitive. Although he never said so, he probably used Jim Brown as a measuring stick for his own athletic success. By that measuring stick or any other, Ernie's career statistics were impressive. His career 6.6 yards per carry average is still the Syracuse benchmark. At the end of the 1961 season, Ernie responded to questions about how he felt breaking Jim Brown's standards. "I never thought of breaking Brown's records this year. Maybe 15 years or so from now, I'll look back and feel proud of the accomplishment." The following is a comparison of the two All-Americans' career statistics:

Davis		Brown
360	Rushing carries	361
2,386	Rushing yardage	2,091
6.6	Rushing average	5.8
38	Pass receptions	11
392	Pass reception yardage	120
5/7	Passing	3/6
110	Passing yardage	76
2,496	Total offense yardage	2,167
6.8	Total offense average per play	5.9
196	Kick-off return yardage	611
224	Punt return yardage	228
5	Interceptions	8
106	Interception yardage	99
35	Touchdowns	25
220	Total points scored	187
3,414	Total yards gained (all ways)	3,225

Ernie Davis played in his last game for Syracuse University in Philadelphia at the Liberty Bowl game on December 16, 1961. It was the Orangemen's second bowl appearance during Ernie's three year varsity career. Syracuse was a six-point favorite over the University of Miami Hurricanes in the cold and windy City of Brotherly Love. The underdogs were led by sophomore quarterback George Mira, a future All-American, who had passed for 896 yards and eight touchdowns during the 1961 season.

As the Heisman Trophy winner and number one pick in the National Football League draft Ernie was the center of a publicity maelstrom prior to the game. Sandy Grady wrote this description of Ernie during Liberty Bowl preparations:

This is the All-American in the most classic, flamboyant sense. When he walks through the Sheraton lobby, lithe and wide-shouldered in his Syracuse blazer, Ernie Davis could not be more revered had he invented a new serum or settled the

Berlin Crisis. Autograph pads form a tunnel for him and
telephones ring in a concert around him—calls from men in
Washington and Cleveland who note Ernie Davis' every opinion as gravely as though he were Adlai Stevenson.

When questioned about the publicity he responded,
"No, all this is no chore to me. I enjoy it. I know it's only
going to happen once." John Mackey remembered, "He
told me to always sign autographs because one day, 'you'll
miss it when they stop asking.' "

Prior to the game Miami coach Andy Gustafson described what it was like to play against Ernie Davis. "Why, I
would have no right to expect my boys to stop Davis for one
entire afternoon. He runs more wrinkles than (Doc)
Blanchard and he's bigger, too." (Gustafson coached
Blanchard at Army).

"You've got to give Syracuse six points every time Davis
walks on the field. We may stop him six or seven times in a
row but he'll get you on the eighth or ninth. The only way
to beat Ernie Davis is to score a lot of points."

Only 15,712 fans attended what turned out to be an
interesting game, one in which each team dominated a
half. The nationally televised event was like two different
games. The Hurricanes jumped out to a 14–0 halftime
lead and did what their coach hadn't anticipated, by holding Davis to 38 yards on ten carries during the first 30
minutes. Dick Easterly and Ernie Davis rallied the Orangemen in the second half for a 15–14 victory. Coach Schwartzwalder recalled, "Ernie won that game practically single
handed. He was the guy gaining the ground so we just let
him have it."

After the game it was learned that Ernie had hurt his
back in the first half and used a heating pad for relief
during intermission. It must have worked because he and
the other Orangemen came out hot for the second half.
Over the last two quarters the Heisman Trophy winner
gained 102 yards on 20 carries and scored his team's first
touchdown on a one-yard plunge. It was his defense at the
end of the game that preserved the victory. In the final

seconds Mira threw a bomb to All-American end Bill Miller which Ernie batted away at the Syracuse 13 yard line.

Dick Easterly was named the game's MVP, and Ernie was selected the best back. In the locker room Ernie commented, "I played sloppy in the first half, as the whole team did. The coach didn't say anything. He was silent, so we all knew we had to go out and play good ball and win." After learning he had 30 carries, he said, "That's the most I ever carried, but I could have carried 20 more without being tired."

The New York Times columnist Arthur Daley quoted Ernie, " 'The team blocked the best ever,' he said, [while Ernie was] happily, thanking everyone for something he had done entirely on his own."

Sandy Grady wrote:

> Anybody can be born unlucky. Some are born rich. A very few are born gifted. But for anybody who ran a football across the autumn backyards in his ripped pants youth, or sweated through endless pushups with a high school jayvee team, it seemed far more worthwhile today to be Ernie Davis.

Number One

December 1961 was probably the high point of Ernie's life. In that month he was presented with the Heisman Trophy, the first black college football player to be so honored. It was a significant racial breakthrough at a time when segregation was just beginning to become the dominant social issue, and American Blacks were recording "firsts" in all areas of life.

When notified of his selection, Ernie's reaction was typically modest. "Winning the Heisman Trophy," he said, "is something you just dream about. You never think it could happen to you. Naturally I always wanted to win it, but I never thought I would." He went on to thank others for his achievement. "Though it's the thrill of a lifetime, I'm not forgetting the many people who helped me win it."

Today, the fact that nine consecutive black athletes have won makes it hard to appreciate what Ernie's achievement meant to his contemporaries. In the eleven years following Ernie's winning the trophy only three other blacks won, Mike Garrett of USC in 1965, O.J. Simpson of USC in 1968, and Johnny Rodgers of Nebraska in 1972. John Mackey summed up the importance of Ernie's winning, "It meant a hell of a lot to blacks. Prior to that we didn't zero in on it because we never thought we'd get it."

Some contend that over the years many outstanding black football players like Buddy Young, Ollie Matson, Jim Brown, or Dick Bass might have won the trophy earlier if they had had an equal opportunity. Georgetown University basketball coach John Thompson raised this notion of opportunity with regard to his own career. In March 1982 he became the "first black coach" to lead his team to the NCAA Final Four. He objected to being characterized in that fashion, stating that it implied that he was the first with the ability and the intelligence to do it. "There were others before me who didn't have the opportunity to try," he maintained.

Winning the Heisman Trophy was an accomplishment Ernie was proud of but it did not dominate his thoughts. The lawyer Tony DeFilippo said, "It would never bother Ernie Davis whether he won the Heisman Trophy or didn't win it. He never discussed it with me. That kid never looked for anything. All he ever thought was, 'What can I do for you?'"

Ernie discussed the Heisman Trophy with Chuck Davis. "He never talked about winning it himself," Davis recalled. "We had a conversation about it on the phone just before the announcement. He felt Bob Ferguson [a black fullback] from Ohio State would win. I argued Jimmy Saxton from Texas would win because only whites won the Heisman Trophy."

After he had been informed of his selection, Ernie called Chuck and identified himself as the white who won the Heisman Trophy. Chuck refused to believe it, but Ernie finally convinced him. Later in the day an excited Chuck told a co-worker the news and the man replied, "He's pulling your leg. He didn't win the Heisman Trophy." Chuck wasn't sure until he heard it on the news that evening.

Ernie was the 27th recipient of the trophy presented annually by the Downtown Athletic Club (DAC) of New York. When Jay Berwanger of the University of Chicago won the first award in 1935 it was not called the Heisman

Trophy. In 1936 the trophy was named in honor of John W. Heisman, Director of Athletics of the DAC who coached at eight colleges and was twice president of the American Football Coaches Association. Ernie was the first resident of New York state to receive the trophy and the third player in four years from the East, following Pete Dawkins of Army in 1958 and Joe Bellino of Navy in 1960.

The voting was done by a panel of 840 sportswriters and sportscasters from all over the country. The final tabulation had Ernie in first place just ahead of Bob Ferguson with Jimmy Saxton third. In fourth place was Ernie's boyhood friend from Uniontown, Pennsylvania, Sandy Stephens, a quarterback from the University of Minnesota. The final ten included four players who became outstanding professionals, John Hadl, Gary Collins, Roman Gabriel and Merlin Olsen.

His senior season had not been Ernie's best in terms of statistics, although he led the Orangemen in rushing with 823 yards, in scoring with 94 points, and in receiving with 16 receptions. Many associated with Syracuse football felt his spectacular sophomore season was also considered by the voters. Coach Schwartzwalder said, "He had three great years. They just didn't dare not give it to him after that third year. It was tribute to his three years really, rather than just one."

Critics have contended that voting for the Heisman Trophy award is unduly influenced by the publicity for major contenders organized by their college athletic departments. One of the most publicized campaigns occurred in 1980 when the University of Pittsburgh Sports Information Director mailed 4,000 color posters of linebacker Hugh Green to members of the media. Green finished second, the highest placement by lineman since John Hicks of Ohio State who was second in 1973. Another case concerned a supposedly anonymous donation of $25,000 to the University of Richmond for the purpose of promoting running back Barry Redden for the Heisman in 1981. The University of Georgia promoted Herschel Walker, the

1982 winner, with a 20 minute film clip including comments by Fran Tarkenton and Tony Dorsett.

It has been estimated that some schools have spent as much as $50,000 promoting a candidate. The estimate is plausible considering the value of the publicity a candidate generates for his school. Television appearances and bowl game invitations can result. The University of South Carolina had never appeared on national television until 1980 winner George Rogers senior year. It was worth $265,000, and their Gator Bowl appearance that season earned another $450,000. It has been estimated that during Walker's three year career Georgia made $10 million. While the impact of all this on the voting can be debated, there seems to be little doubt that major colleges have publicized star players with the hope of promoting their chances for the Heisman Trophy.

There seems to have been little of this in Ernie's case, if for no other reason than that no one thought seriously about promoting a black player for the trophy. Val Pinchbeck, then Syracuse University's Sports Information Director and now Director of Broadcasting for the NFL, said:

> There was no concerted campaign of any sort to get the Heisman Trophy for Ernie Davis. Not in any degree the way it is now. If you campaigned, you campaigned for a guy to make All-American. I did nothing different for Ernie Davis at that point than I did for Jimmy Brown, Floyd Little, John Mackey, or any of the others.

While he was in New York for the ceremonies, Ernie was applauded, interviewed, and televised with the intensity usually accorded national heroes. President John F. Kennedy was in the city at the time and asked to see Ernie, who was thrilled by the President's request.

The meeting was an improvised affair that took place only because of the persistence of the two parties. When first notified that President Kennedy wanted to see him, Ernie was attending a banquet in his honor. Carrying the 25 pound trophy, Ernie rushed out with Pinchbeck and a DAC official and hailed a cab for the Carlyle Hotel where the President was staying. They were held up due to security regulations, so by the time they arrived, all they saw was a fleeting glimpse of Kennedy as he was driven away.

Disappointed, they returned to the luncheon. No sooner had they started eating than another call came from the President. He was now at the Waldorf Astoria Hotel and wanted to meet Ernie there. This time they were successful. Pinchbeck described the meeting.

> We're standing in an anteroom talking when the doors open and here comes the President. He walked up and introduced himself, "Hi, I'm Jack Kennedy." They chatted and the President remarked what an honor it was to win the Heisman Trophy. A picture was taken and we left.

At the time of Ernie's death, sports columnist Arthur Daley wrote, "When the President greeted Ernie, he shook hands with one of his finest citizens."

Coach Schwartzwalder, who saw Ernie shortly after he had seen the President, recalled Ernie's reaction. "He practicaly knocked me down. He went clear across the lobby and he had his hand out. He said, 'Put 'er there, Coach. Put 'er there. That's the hand that shook hands with President Kennedy.' He was so elated that President Kennedy bothered to say hello to him. It was like he won a lottery for a million dollars. He was so fired up. I sat and talked to him for 15 or 20 minutes. He just couldn't get over it."

At a press conference, a smiling Ernie stated, "I missed my lunch, but it doesn't matter. It was the greatest thrill of my life—that and winning the Heisman Trophy. Imagine the President wanting to shake hands with me." He had, in fact, come a long way. Teammate John Brown recalled, "He went from nothing to meeting the President of the United States. You have to think about that. He handled it well."

That evening 1,100 people attended the Heisman Trophy presentation banquet at the DAC. The Mutual Broadcasting radio network system broadcast live from 10-10:30 p.m. as club president, Clifford E. Deming, presented the trophy to Ernie. His acceptance speech was a modest thanks to his mother, Syracuse University, his coaches, and his teammates. His mother proudly recalled the event.

> I had no idea what he was going to say in his acceptance speech. He never expressed himself to me before in that manner. It was more or less about the part I played in his life along with other people for him to reach the goal he had reached in winning the Heisman Trophy. I guess I took it a little different than other people.

Schwartzwalder recalled, "Most of his speech was just thanking everyone. He'd be the last guy to ever say that he did anything. He never talked about Ernie, just people and other things. He loved everything that was wholesome and good. You never had any trouble talking with Ernie. He just bubbled over."

The veteran Syracuse equipment manager Al Zak, upon hearing Ernie won the Heisman Trophy said, "Ernie still wears the same 7¼ hat size that I outfitted him with when he walked in here as a frosh. Even now, you'd never even know the kid was around."

Ernie's mother with Tony DeFilippo's encouragement donated Ernie's Heisman Trophy to Syracuse University in 1963. Today the athlete's college receives a replica. The trophy was displayed in a case under his portrait in the lobby of Manley Fieldhouse until 1980 when it was moved to the Ernie Davis Memorial Room in the Carrier Dome, the university's new football stadium.

One April Fool's day in the early 1970s the trophy was stolen from the fieldhouse display but returned shortly thereafter, demonstrating the award's value. If it's not yours what can you do with it? Since 1935 there have been thousands of college football players, hundreds of All-Americans, but only 48 Heisman Trophy winners. There are not many more exclusive groups in the country.

Over the next eight months Ernie reached the pinnacle of his career and became one of the most heralded college football players. During that period Ernie lived the All-American dream. He was the first player selected in the National Football League draft, signed a then league record-setting rookie contract, played in post season games around the country; and was in great demand on the banquet circuit.

He kept the media attention in perspective, saying that God had given him the ability to achieve what he had. He never felt he was owed the adulation, but he accepted it modestly. Sportswriter Sandy Grady described Ernie at the time,

> The smile never leaves Ernie Davis' face. He must wear it in his sleep. It's the half-surprised, amused, secret smile of a man aware that something immensely pleasant will happen to him. Ernie Davis is right. The pros can't wait to shower him with gold and promises, and the fame will probably go on and on.

The professional football league drafts for 1962 were conducted behind smokescreens of publicity. The Newspaper accounts did not always coincide with the private dealings. As the number one college player in the country, Ernie was the subject of intense interest. What teams would draft him? Which league would sign him? How much money would he receive? While the pros were looking out for their personal interests, Ernie and his hometown lawyer, Tony DeFilippo, were looking out for Ernie's. Regardless of the publicity, they had the negotiations under control.

The college football draft, when Ernie was eligible, was very different than today's draft. In December 1961, there were two opposing leagues, the established National Football League and the fledgling American Football League, competing for college players and fan support. Professional football's popularity had not yet been established. The sold-out stadiums and record television contracts of today did not exist. Today's newly formed United States Football League does not pose the same challenge as the old AFL. The USFL's draft and season are not in direct competition with the NFL.

The two leagues held separate collegiate drafts in which the outstanding college players were drafted by teams in each league. The drafts were held immediately after the college season to enable teams to sign players as quickly as possible to avoid loosing them to the rival league. The professional season was still in progress. Today the draft is conducted in the spring to give pro teams more time to scout potential draftees. There was no competition between the two leagues on the field, but it was intense in draftee contract negotiations. To insure credibility, the NFL teams felt they had to sign the top players, while to establish credibility, the AFL teams felt they must also sign the best prospects.

In an effort to achieve these goals, teams from each league offered unprecedented salaries, bonuses, and perks to top draft choices. The resulting contract bidding war was nearly fatal to both the NFL and the AFL and was a significant factor in the eventual merger of the two leagues. The common draft of today was a major result of the merger.

In a column written at the time of Ernie's death, Arthur Daley of *The New York Times*, revealed a story which demonstrated how highly Ernie was regarded as a pro prospect.

> The far-seeing New York Giants had their eyes fixed on Ernie when he was a junior at Syracuse. On the assumption that the newly formed Minnesota Vikings would be in last place when Ernie was eligible for the draft, Wellington Mara traded George Shaw to the Vikings for a first round draft choice a year later. He was to be Davis.

However, the Giants' plan regarding Davis fell through when their need for a pass receiver became paramount. They traded the draft choice to the Rams for Del Shofner, who helped lead them to a championship.

As far as the public was aware, the Washington Redskins, the team with the worst record in the league, had the initial selection in the December 4th NFL draft. However, prior to the draft, the Redskins had in fact traded the choice to the Cleveland Browns for Bobby Mitchell, a four-year veteran halfback, and also one of the Browns' two number one choices in the draft. The trade was not immediately announced because the Browns had regular season games remaining and wanted to play Mitchell. As the number one college player selected in the draft, Cleveland wanted Ernie Davis, so the Redskins drafted him for the Browns. As part of the trade, Washington wanted halfback Leroy Jackson of Western Illinois, so the Browns picked him for the

Redskins with their second number one draft choice. Without a public announcement of the trade, Washington fans mistakenly looked forward to seeing Ernie Davis in a Redskins uniform. Before the draft, Art Modell, President of the Cleveland Browns called Tony DeFilippo. He informed the lawyer that the Cleveland Browns had the number one pick and would use it to select Ernie Davis. DeFilippo was skeptical and wanted proof of the deal. At Modell's urging, he contacted Washington owner George Preston Marshall, who verified the trade agreement.

From the outset of the negotiating period, DeFilippo had resolved not to become involved in a bidding war between the two leagues for Ernie's services. A neophyte in professional football contract negotiations, DeFilippo sought advice from both pro and college personnel experts. He wanted to determine how good Ernie was and how much he was worth to the pros. The response he received was encouraging. The conventional wisdom of the experts was also reassuring. Bucko Kilroy, then a scout with the Philadelphia Eagles, was quoted in the newspapers as saying, "Davis will be more spectacular than in college because the defenses in the pros can't afford to be stacked toward stopping him as they were in college."

With their new information, DeFilippo and Ernie put together a $250,000 no-cut, no-trade contract package. The proposal was ambitious for the times. Earlier Ernie had expressed the hope that he could get a $20,000 contract. After the proposal was finalized, DeFilippo instructed Ernie not to talk terms with anyone. He explained, "I didn't want to get into a bidding war—asking $10,000 from this guy and $10,000 more from that guy."

The contract proposal was then presented to Modell and later to Ralph C. Wilson, owner of the Buffalo Bills. There had been reports of offers from Canada, but DeFilippo used this as a ruse and never negotiated with any Canadian teams. Modell initially balked at the no-cut no-trade provision, saying NFL Commissioner Pete Rozelle would not approve such a clause. DeFilippo responded, "Rozelle will do anything you owners want him to do." The provision remained in the contract. DeFilippo explained the reason for the clause. "We didn't want him traded to another team for somebody else's profit. If anybody was going to make money off Ernie, it was going to be Ernie."

Ernie was not the player the Browns most coveted in their early pre-draft meetings. Initially, discussion centered on quarterback Roman Gabriel and fullback Bob Ferguson. At Ernie's signing ceremony, Modell recalled, "We were after relief for [Jim] Brown, who had taken an unmerciful beating for five years. Finally we came around to Davis and we decided he was the player who could give us exactly what we wanted—someone to take the pressure off Brown, one who had speed and could block."

Over 20 years later Modell explained why the Browns wanted Ernie, "Our scouts were convinced Davis and Brown would make the greatest backfield ever."

In his autobiography, then Cleveland Coach Paul Brown wrote, "As the 1961 season wound down, we began discussions with the Redskins about trading Bobby Mitchell as part of a deal to get Ernie Davis. . .The entire staff was thoroughly convinced that a team in our climate needed two big fast runners to overcome the rough playing conditions late in the season. . ."

Before, during and after the NFL draft, the words and actions of the top Redskins management seemed to preclude a trade. The Redskins were the only racially segregated team in the NFL. "Burgundy, gold and Caucasian," were the Redskins' team colors wrote *The Washington Post's* Shirley Povich. He also noted, "The Redskins' color line was stronger than their offensive and defensive lines." The team's fight song Hail to the Redskins' originally contained the line, 'Cheer for Old Dixie.' It was rewritten as 'Fight for Old D.C.' "

The racial policies of team owner George Preston Marshall attracted the attention of the Kennedy Administration. The fall of 1961 was the Redskins first in the city's new District of Columbia Stadium, now named for Robert F. Kennedy. Since the stadium was built with federal funds

A familiar sight to opponents, #44 running for a long gain (Courtesy Chuck Davis)

Ernie during varsity basketball action (Courtesy Chuck Davis)

Ernie demonstrates his speed, leaving defenders behind (Courtesy Chuck Davis)

To the cheers of the crowd, Davis races for his third touchdown (Courtesy Chuck Davis)

In action at Archbold Stadium (Courtesy Chuck Davis)

Looking for an opening as the defense surrounds him (Courtesy Chuck Davis)

on land controlled by the U.S. Department of the Interior, the government could apply political pressure. To avoid a confrontation, the Redskins made a complicated series of maneuvers which brought the first black football player to Washington, although not Ernie Davis.

The Kennedy Administration was committed to the policy that every American should have an equal opportunity to use his or her talents in all aspects of our national life. So in March 1961, Secretary of the Interior, Stewart Udall, ordered Marshall to hire black athletes or be barred from using D.C. Stadium for the upcoming season. In response, Marshall denied his team practiced segregation, stating, "We've had a Samoan, a Hawaiian, Indians, and a Cuban, but no Negroes."

Marshall won a postponement of the ban to the following season because there would be no college draft between March and the opening of the 1961 season in which to sign players, and because Marshall wrote a letter to NFL Commissioner Pete Rozelle in which he promised to make every effort to draft one or more blacks in the December draft for the 1962 season. In the letter to Rozelle, Marshall declared, "The Redskins have no policy against hiring of football players because of their race." The sole aim of his club he insisted "was to continue to field a team that will represent Washington, D.C. in the National Football League." The owner also indicated he hoped to draft either Ernie or Ohio State fullback, Bob Ferguson.

Shirley Povich wrote on November 11, 1961:

> Intergrated pro football long ago was accepted by the players and the fans. Marshall has been the only holdout. He has keyed the Redskins promotion to his Southern radio-TV network to exploit Nordic supremacy which in the case of the Redskins has been nil for seventeen games in a row. Washington has been able to cheer one victory in two years.

Povich also noted that the Redskins, "need the lease on the new stadium which, to date, has proven more of a fan attraction than the football team."

At a November 27th press conference, questions concerning the upcoming draft were asked of Marshall and head coach Bill McPeak. They stated eight different teams had contacted them concerning a trade for the number one choice and McPeak was asked if he would forgo drafting Ernie Davis. Marshall responded: "That question should be directed to me because I'm responsible for this team. But I shall defer to the coach. He may make a deal or he may not. It's up to him. Naturally, as owner, I would insist upon being consulted before any final decision is made."

The owner was asked if the Redskins would select black players in the upcoming draft as promised. He answered, "If we take a Negro, it will be because we think he is the best pick. It won't be because a player is a Negro." Concerning a trade, McPeak indicated he would be receptive to offers although he was admittedly high on Ernie as a prospect. He stated, "We will have to get Davis or a back of similar ability."

On draft day, Washington went through with the charade of drafting Ernie Davis, but many football experts were skeptical. When the Browns, with the fourth choice, selected Maryland's All-American end Gary Collins from Washington's backyard, the rumors of a trade between the two teams increased.

The most popular scenario had Ernie going to Cleveland for Collins and Mitchell, who was on active duty in the United States Army at Fort Meade, Maryland. President Kennedy had activated some army reserve units for the Berlin Crisis in 1961, and many professional athletes who were reservists were called to active duty. Paul Brown, the Cleveland coach, scotched that rumor, "We are going to keep Collins. Obviously we like him. He's going to play end for us and do our punting. How does this nonsense start?"

Later, on draft day, it was the same Coach Brown who gave the first official indication that a trade between the two teams might be worked out. "It involves a couple of problems," the coach said. "All I can say is that if we are able to work something out, we'll be glad to get Davis. We need protection at running halfback."

Vince Lombardi, the Green Bay Packers coach and general manager, commented to Brown at the draft, "If the rumors I've heard are true, you've made the greatest deal of the year—no, century. If it's true, I hope I don't have to play you for another 15 years. He's worth anything he cost you."

After the draft, Washington management sought to allay the media speculation concerning a trade. Coach Bill McPeak said, "We picked Ernie Davis number one. That's the story. We're not responsible for wild speculation. Obviously we like Davis. I have high hopes we will sign him." In Washington, Marshall responded to a question about his ability to sign Ernie by saying, "I think its no problem." Regarding the speculation of a trade having been consummated, he replied, "I couldn't say so." He did, however, again indicate the Redskins would be willing to listen to trade offers.

In the meantime, public enthusiasm over the prospect of Ernie Davis in a Redskins uniform was supported by members of the press and prominent Washingtonians unaware a trade had been consummated. On December 6th, *The Washington Post* sports columnist Bob Addie wrote, "The Redskins would be pretty stupid to trade away Ernie Davis. That's the most talked about draft choice Washington ever made and local fans are excited about seeing the Syracuse star in action here."

Shirley Povich wrote:

> Davis is the hottest football property to come out of the colleges in years. Davis appears to be the player most needed by the Redskins, and in drafting him, the Redskins tacitly made it an article of faith with Redskins fans that he would be signed. It's a gratuitous thing to tell others how much money to spend, but the bidding for Davis has begun and despite the Redskins failure to win any of their last 22, this could be one contest they can't afford to lose.

Redskins general manager, Dick McCann, announced that the Washington business community was rallying behind the effort to sign Ernie. McCann said, "They've offered him everything but a membership in Burning Tree," an exclusive golf course where former President Eisenhower used to play. The offers included a radio sports show, a sales position with a liquor distributor, and a clothes consultant. "I don't think most of the offers are an attempt to capitalize on the boy either," McCann said. "They represent a sincere desire on the part of business-men who just want Davis to play for the Redskins and to see the team improved." According to the local news-papers, prominent Washington attorney Edward Bennett Williams prevailed upon black Congressman Adam Clayton Powell of New York to telephone Ernie on behalf of Williams and the Redskins. Tony DeFilippo, however, said he was not aware of any conversations Ernie had with Powell or Williams about a contract. "If he had any," said DeFilippo, "he would have told me, I'm sure." After all the publicity, it would seem logical that the Redskins would make every effort to have Ernie Davis the number one pick and Heisman Trophy winner as the team's first black player unless he had been traded.

The AFL draft on December 2nd was also controversial and did not proceed according to the script some had anticipated. It became public that two weeks ahead of schedule the AFL owners had conducted a secret tele-phone draft of six rounds. The National Collegiate Ath-letic Association (NCAA), which had an agreement with the two leagues banning the drafting of college players until the end of the regular season, was outraged. It was similar to the controversy which developed in 1981 when the USFL drafted Heisman Trophy winner Herschel Walker of Georgia who still had a year of college eligibility. As a result of the adverse publicity, AFL Commissioner Joe Foss declared the premature draft "null and void." Harry Wismer, the voluble owner of the New York Titans (now Jets), however, stated he would "go along as if the draft is official." In an angry tirade, he stated, "I am going to extend every effort to bring to the Titans the players we have drafted and will have a contract for them the second they become eligible to play professional football. I will pay more than anyone else for their services." Wismer publically announced that Ernie was the number one choice among the six players the Titans hoped to sign.

On the eve of the AFL draft, Wismer announced he was prepared to offer Ernie an unprecedented $100,000 three-year, no-cut contract with an additional $25,000 signing bonus. The owner said, "If anybody wants to top that, I'll top what they want to offer. The contract will be waiting at the dressing room (after the Liberty Bowl) for Davis." Wismer felt it was imperative to sign a player of Ernie's caliber in order to establish the new league's credibility. Three years later, Wismer helped secure the AFL's future by signing Alabama quarterback, Joe Namath.

The scenario at the official AFL draft did not proceed as Wismer had envisioned. The Buffalo Bills, picking just ahead of Wismer's Titans, drafted Ernie on the first round, as the fourth player selected. This was the first deviation from the voided secret draft and caught the Titans off guard. Their general manager, Steve Sebo, clashed with Foss and protested, claiming that Ernie was the Titans' man. With his protests falling on deaf ears, Sebo borrowed a dime to make a long distance phone call to Wismer in New York. After a half hour, he could not get through, and Foss ordered the draft to continue. The Titans then selected Minnesota quarterback Sandy Stephens.

Later, during the morning session, Sebo protested again that the secret draft should be sustained. "That's impossible," Foss declared. "Davis has been drafted by Buffalo." Unwilling to completely give up his quest for Ernie, Wismer declared that evening that he would do "everything possible" to make a deal for Ernie Davis. The owner had declared Davis had been anxious to sign the previously announced $125,000 three-year, no-cut contract with the Titans. "I asked him, 'Are you satisfied?' " Wismer said. Davis supposedly answered, "Yes, very much so." As with the Redskins pronouncements, DeFilippo declared there was never any contract negotiations with Wismer or the

Titans. "I told Ernie not to discuss money with any of these guys. I didn't want them bidding back and forth in the newspapers."

The Buffalo Bills, owned by millionaire Ralph C. Wilson, were not about to concede Ernie without a battle. The Bills general manager, Dick Gallagher announced that he had a meeting scheduled in Elmira with DeFilippo. He stated, "It may be weeks or months before we can sign Davis, but we can't afford to lose him. Davis means too much to football and the entire upstate [New York] area."

A former Cleveland Browns official, Gallagher had played a prominent role in the signing of Jim Brown. The general manager said, "In the several talks I've had with Ernie, he talked about the fine job Brown had in the off-season with a soft drink company. I told him I'm sure we could do as well." With regard to a possible bidding war with Washington over Ernie's services, Gallagher declared, "Whatever the Redskins offer, the Bills will match or surpass."

After the meeting with DeFilippo on December 11th, Gallagher told newsmen, "No negotiations will be held until a much later date. We just wanted to know a little more about Ernie." The general manager also denied reports that the Bills had relinquished rights to Ernie to the New York Titans. The Bills owner, Ralph C. Wilson, also refuted a statement by Titans owner Harry Wismer that he had been given permission by Buffalo to negotiate with Ernie. Wilson declared, "We drafted him with the intention of signing him and still intend to."

During this time Ernie was in New York City as a member of the 1961 *Look* magazine All-America team. Val Pinchbeck, the Syracuse Sports Information Director, remembered Ernie taking him aside prior to a press conference and advising him not to worry if Ernie was not entirely forthcoming about this future pro career. He knew he had been traded by the Redskins to Cleveland, he informed Pinchbeck.

At the press conference, Pinchbeck recalled:

A writer asked Ernie if he would go with the AFL or the NFL? He answered to the effect that he would do what was best for his future. He said he'd talk to the Bills and see what they'd offer. It won't be exclusively a money decision. "I'm going to talk to Cleveland, I mean, I'm going to talk to Washington." No one ever picked up on it.

On December 14th the rumors and speculation concerning a trade of Ernie were substantiated. Both clubs confirmed that they had, in fact, negotiated the trade prior to the draft. Cleveland received the NFL rights to sign Ernie while the Redskins acquired one of the Browns two number-one draft choices, Leroy Jackson, and a veteran to be named "on or before February 1, 1962." Jackson played two seasons with the team. The identity of the veteran player immediately became known, Bobby Mitchell, who went on to become a member of the Pro Football Hall of Fame and is currently an assistant general manager of the Redskins.

According to Cleveland coach Paul Brown, Redskins owner George Preston Marshall wanted Mitchell to break his team's color line. "Marshall knew that Bobby was a class person, very intelligent, and low key, and felt he was probably the only player who could handle the special situation," wrote Brown. "I discussed all this with Bobby beforehand and allowed him to discuss the situation with Marshall. He foresaw no problems, so it came down to structuring the trade."

Bobby Mitchell had an entirely different recollection of the famous trade. He recalled, "I was stationed at Ft. Meade, Maryland, and John Paluck, a Redskins defensive end, was also stationed there. Every morning he'd say to me, 'Something big's about to happen.' I eventually figured out it was me being traded to Washington. He had heard about it somehow."

The suspense and speculation which affected the media and the fans did not concern Mitchell.

Two games before the end of the season I knew something was up because I wasn't being used except to return kicks. Paul Brown came up to my locker after the last game but couldn't say anything to me. Till this day nobody from the Cleveland Browns ever told me officially I was traded. Mr. Marshall just called me up and said he wanted to see me. I already had a contract so we didn't even have to negotiate. He always treated me fairly.

Initially Mitchell was treated unfairly by the fans, and he became the object of verbal abuse. Once while dining in a famous Washington Restaurant, Mitchell was spit upon. He let his performances on the field do his talking for him and eventually became a favorite of the team's fans.

Since the bidding war for draft choices between the NFL and the AFL had begun, it was not uncommon to have top draft choices sign contracts under the goalpost or in the locker room immediately following the player's last game. The Liberty Bowl had many exciting moments, but one thing it didn't have was Ernie Davis signing a contract.

In Philadelphia, after the game Ernie explained, "I will not make a decision on which pro team I'll go to until at least two weeks. I may even wait until after the East-West game [December 30]." Grinning, he admitted money might be a factor, "I have to make a living, so it's whoever makes the best offer."

Ernie proved to be a poor prognosticator because he agreed to a contract with the Cleveland Browns five days later and for less money than the Buffalo Bills offered. Art Modell announced Ernie had accepted a three-year, no-cut, no-trade $65,000 contract with a $15,000 signing bonus. At the time the contract was the largest ever given a rookie in the history of the NFL.

The contract was actually more lucrative than publicly announced, as in addition, Ernie also signed two other contracts. They were both ten year contracts; one, $60,000 for ancilliary rights and the other $60,000 for off season employment. Each contract was guaranteed and for tax purposes deferred. Explained DeFilippo, "If Ernie made more than $60,000, he could keep it. Modell could recoup the first $60,000."

Coach Paul Brown wrote this account of the contract negotiations:

I talked to Ernie first and knew from my conversation that Buffalo didn't have much of a chance, but I made a specific point again of advising Art Modell, who had never done this before, that we had a policy against no-cut contracts, regardless of the player situation, and that we never announced salary terms because that created problems with other players. Modell deliberately went against my wishes, however, and the newspapers soon splashed the news that Ernie had an $80,000 no-cut contract.

Throughout the negotiations, Ernie had stated that his future after football was an important consideration. Ernie realized he couldn't play forever and wanted to insure he had a career and financial stability to fall back on once he left the game. The Browns had agreed to assist him by setting up a series of vocational skills tests. When the agreement was announced, Ernie stated, "I hope to learn a business during the off season and step into a good job after 8 to 10 years in the National Football League."

The contract Ernie signed was $50,000 less than the $250,000 tendered by the Buffalo Bills. According to De-Filippo, their tax gimmick was also better, but Ernie chose to play with the Browns because of the NFL, Modell and Jim Brown. Ernie confirmed that Buffalo offered more money, "But it wasn't enough to offset the other things involved." He explained, "A player has pride and wants to play with the best. I don't mean to knock the other league. Maybe in a couple of years it will be different." Now Modell dismisses the threat posed by the AFL Buffalo Bills signing Davis, "We were determined to sign him."

At the contract signing an excited Modell said, "There just aren't enough words to express my happiness now that Ernie has decided to play with us. It's certainly gratifying to know that young athletes like Davis consider their long-range future rather than immediate financial gain." Agreeing to terms with Cleveland fulfilled a childhood dream of Ernie's. "As a youngster, I always wanted to play with the Browns or the New York Giants. But a couple of years ago I realized it really didn't matter which team I played with."

The actual contract signing occurred on Thursday, December 28, 1961 at the Fairmont Hotel in San Francisco, where Ernie was practicing for the East-West Shrine All-Star game. In response to a question, Ernie reached into his pocket and revealed he had sixteen cents and a key. A few seconds later he had $15,000, sixteen cents, and a key. Modell had DeFilippo flown to San Francicsco for the contract signing. The lawyer recalled, "After the ceremony, Ernie and I toured San Francisco in a limo provided by Art Modell."

Bob Brachman of the *San Francisco Examiner* wrote this account of the proceedings:

> It was the All-American boy story at its most heart warming. Reared by his mother, a $55-a-week matron in a precision tool plant at Elmira, New York. Ernie whispered a silent prayer of thanks as Modell handed him the first installment. He fondled the check, turned it over and over as if making certain it was real and then said simply, "I'm sending it home to pay off all my mother's obligations. I never thought this could happen," he said, displaying the record-making document for newsmen and photographers. "It's going to be quite an honor playing alongside Jim Brown."

Regarding the bonus, Ernie's mother recalled, "We had many a footstep to our door telling us what to do with the money. After buying some things, the rest went in the bank."

The Browns' trade with Washington for Ernie Davis was not contingent upon their signing Ernie. At an East-West game press luncheon, East coach Bill Murray of Duke introduced Ernie, "Paul Brown gave away a star and a number one draft choice just for the right to talk to Davis." Modell indicated he felt no risk in signing a rookie to such a large contract. He said, "We think we have a great player for 8 or 9 years." In jest he added, "If he doesn't make it, he will be the most expensive equipment manager of all time." The board chairman of the Browns said he released the contract figures "because we wanted to put an end to the wild speculation about how much Davis was getting." He, in fact, announced only part of the package. Modell went to San Francisco for the contract signing because Ernie would be going directly to the Hula Bowl in Hawaii and wouldn't be back in the East until mid-January. "As for the $15,000, we wanted Ernie to have it now," he said, "so it would go on the current calendar year income tax report. That'll save him something." The tax bite was approximately $4,000.

The East-West game, nicknamed "the game with a heart", is an annual charity benefit for the Shriners Hospital for Crippled Children. During training camps, members of both squads visit the children at the hospital. Ernie brought his camera and was a big hit with the kids. John McDaniel, writing in the *San Francisco Examiner*, wrote a touching account of a meeting between Ernie and one of the children.

> Ernie Davis is a bull necked, steel shouldered All-American halfback from Syracuse University who can run a football field's length in something less than 10 seconds flat. Kathy is a tawny haired ten-year-old from San Jose with laughing blue eyes, a smile like sunshine, and legs that can't carry her down the hall. And one thing they have in common is—courage. . . .
>
> "You're bigger than I thought," Kathy said. "You're pretty," said Davis. Kathy was asked which team she wanted to win the game and Kathy didn't answer for a moment. She looked at Davis, eyes shining and saucer sized. "Don't look at me", said the halfback. "Anything you say is alright with me." But she said the right thing. "Ernie's team will win."

Among those attending the game was Chief Justice of the Supreme Court, Earl Warren, and California Governor Pat Brown. The East squad was favored by 7½ points, but West quarterback John Hadl, the game's MVP, led a 28-8 upset. Ernie was the game's leading rusher with 83 yards on 18 carries and scored a two-point conversion.

Winning the Heisman Trophy and signing a record-breaking professional contract made Ernie a popular personality during the winter banquet circuit of 1961-62. As his fame spread, so did the demands on his time, but he didn't let that affect him. In *The Saturday Evening Post* article shortly before his death he wrote, "I think everybody wants some kind of recognition, something that will make them stand out of a crowd and make people admire them". Daily he received requests for appearances to accept more awards or deliver a speech. Regarding that period, he wrote in the same article, "I found myself leaving college almost every Friday and not getting back to campus until Sunday, traveling all over the East and Midwest. Finally I reached a point where I decided I had to get some time in April. Even then, after graduation in June, I still felt worn down." Another problem with the traveling was that it took time away from his studies. His mother said, "He had to study extra hard. In fact, his last year he had to have a tutor because he was away from school so much."

Ernie overcame his natural reticence and speech difficulty to make these public appearances. As many public speakers do, Ernie used a piece of paper with key phrases written on it as a cue. Friends said that the speeches were short because the papers were so tiny. Chuck Davis always kidded Ernie, "Your speeches are too long. Nobody wants to listen to you." His mother recollected, "He said on many occasions he didn't know how he got through his speeches." In spite of the speeches, Ernie really enjoyed the banquets because they gave him an opportunity to meet new people, which was one of the great satisfactions of his life. Coach Schwartzwalder said:

> He loved people. He'd pet a dog if there was one on the practice field. If there was a three-year old kid, Ernie would talk to him. Some athletes become overwhelmed with autograph seekers and they tire of it. Ernie loved every minute of it, and not because they were paying him tribute, but because he just liked to talk to folks. He'd talk about anything.

Ironically, one of the first banquets he attended that year was in Washington, D.C., on January 13th. The Washington Touchdown Club presented Ernie the Walter Camp Memorial Trophy awarded annually since 1937 to the best college running back in the nation. Other award winners that evening included Vince Lombardi, Paul "Bear" Bryant, Paul Hornung, Whitey Ford, and Stan Musial. Those in attendance included Vice President Lyndon

Johnson, Secretary of State Dean Rusk, Secretary of Labor Arthur Goldberg, and Speaker of the House John McCormack.

Secretary Goldberg presented the Camp Memorial Trophy to Ernie noting, "The Department of Justice has been asleep on this. Now they are standing idly by while Ernie Davis is merging with Jim Brown on the Cleveland team. That's monopoly of the most flagrant kind." *The Washington Post* reporter George Minot wrote the next day: "Ernie Davis of Syracuse, looking clean-cut and trim, like an All-American should, said, 'I'm glad to be with the Cleveland Browns, but I would have played with the Redskins. It's not true what some newspapers said, that I would not have played for Washington.' "

A short time later he was driving from Syracuse to Elmira in a blizzard with teammate Bill Fitzgerald. "Ernie had the trophy he had received in Washington taking up the whole back seat of the car," Fitzgerald recalled. In heavy snow around Cortland, Ernie ran into the back of a car filled with girls who immediately called the State Police to report the accident. When the trooper arrived, he instantly recognized Ernie and insisted he get out of the snow and into the warm patrol car. Fitzgerald said, "The trooper was filling out the accident report and asked, 'Ernie, how far behind the car were you when you hit your brakes?' Nervous, Ernie began to stutter and couldn't answer. The officer said, 'You were at least 120 or 130 feet weren't you?' Ernie quickly nodded affirmatively."

They had the car towed and decided to try to catch the last bus from Cortland. Fitzgerald remembered, "The trooper volunteered to take us. We pulled up to the bus station with the light flashing and the siren blaring. The trooper got out and shook hands with Ernie. Many of the people at the station recognized him so he ended up signing autographs for them and we almost missed the bus." Of all the affairs he attended, the most gratifying had to be the "Elmira Salutes Ernie Davis Day" on Saturday, February 3, 1962. Planning the ceremonies began prior to the announcement that Ernie had won the Heisman Trophy. It was a heartfelt display of affection from the citizens of Elmira to its favorite son. In the morning, Ernie met with the children at the YMCA and was presented with a lifetime membership. That evening 1,500 adults attended the dinner at Notre Dame High School, making it the largest sports banquet in the history of Elmira.

High school basketball coach Jim Flynn recalled a vivid memory from that evening. After the banquet and prior to the speakers, the bleachers in the gym were opened to the general public. Flynn said, "I looked up and saw these older women teachers in their 60's climbing up in the bleachers. I thought what a tribute to a great guy."

Included at the head table were New York Governor Nelson Rockefeller, Jim Brown, Art Modell, and Ben Schwartzwalder. The mood of the evening was light and many of the speakers were humorous. Rockefeller, after noting Ernie had been born in Pennsylvania, joked, "We're sure glad you moved, Ernie." Observing the audience and the dignitaries at the head table, the Governor stated, "I couldn't help thinking, wouldn't it be wonderful if the people behind the Iron Curtain could get a look at this and see what a wonderful country this is, a community turned out in tribute to a young man they know and love." Governor Rockefeller had been sincerely impressed by the warmth of the public outpouring and said to Ernie, "I don't know what you are going to do after school, but let's you and I get together and go into some sort of business."

In brief remarks, Jim Brown stated, "I think Ernie has the potential to come into pro football and repeat what he did in college, namely break my records. Ernie, we are going to welcome you to the Cleveland Browns with open hands." Art Modell, referring to a Rockefeller statement that Ernie is modest and brief in speaking, publicly quipped, "He seemed to recall his eloquence when negotiating a contract." He described the Browns conference at which they decided whom to select in the college draft and added, "One thing we were certain of, we made a smart move in getting Ernie Davis."

The new 1962 Thunderbird presented to Ernie by the citizens of Elmira at "Salute to Ernie Davis Day" on February 3, 1962 (Courtesy Chuck Davis)

Coach Schwartzwalder said: "We at Syracuse feel very fortunate that a boy like Ernie came to Syracuse. We only promised him an opportunity to get an education and play football. Ernie did the rest. When big Jim [Brown] graduated, it was the end of an era. When Ernie graduates, it will be the end of another era. We've been so fortunate to have two superstars."

President John F. Kennedy sent the following telegram,

Seldom has an athlete been more deserving of such a tribute. Your high standards of performance on the field and off the field, reflect the finest qualities of competition, sportsmanship and citizenship. This nation has bestowed on you its highest awards for your athletic achievements. It's a privilege for me to address you tonight as an outstanding American, and as a worthy example of our youth. I salute you.

The toastmaster, Marty Harrigan, Ernie's high-school football coach, had told the audience that Ernie's only athletic shortcoming was an inability to swim. Ernie quickly responded, referring to his lifetime membership at the "Y", "I'll be able to work on that now." In his formal address, Ernie thanked everyone including God "for giving me the body, capabilities, and abilities to do the things I've done."

Relaxed, he chided the audience for paying money to see him when they could see him for free any day on the sidewalk. Then, surveying the head table he surmised the crowd hadn't come to see him after all, but those seated there instead. Among the gifts Ernie received were the keys to a brand new 1962 Thunderbird convertible presented by the community. Ernie joked, "Now I'll have to go to all the gas stations in town." Family and friends recall that Ernie was deeply touched by the event. He couldn't get over the fact that people in Elmira thought enough of him to have such a ceremony.

Ernie loved the Thunderbird and kept it in perfect running condition. On a warm spring day a friend and his girl came by as Ernie was leaving the house. The friend asked if he could test drive the Thunderbird. Assuming he meant a short drive around the block, Ernie said okay. He waited on the sidewalk so long for the driver to return that other friends started to gather. Others drove by and reported they had seen the car in various locations throughout the city. Finally, they returned with the car. Smiling, Ernie walked over to where they had parked and asked how they liked it. "Fine. It really handles nice." As the others gathered around, Ernie said, "I'm glad you enjoyed your two rides in my car." The driver responded, "We didn't have two rides. We had one." Ernie explained, "You had two, your first and your last."

Ernie's pleasure with the Thunderbird may have been enhanced by the bad luck he had had with his first car, a black and white Edsel which had been a legendary disaster at Syracuse.

Ernie had to call friends many times to get the car jump-started. Before consenting to ride anywhere in the Edsel, Chuck Davis would always check to make sure Ernie had

Look Magazine All- American weekend in New York, 1961 (Courtesy Al Mallette)

Coach Swartzwalder hands football to Jim Brown and Ernie at the Elmira Salutes Ernie Davis banquet (Courtesy SU Sports Information)

Party at Chicago Playboy Key Club for pre-season All- American team, (left to right) Hugh Hefner, *Playboy* Publisher, Anson Mount, *Playboy* football forcaster, Fred Mautino, All-American from Syracuse, Davis and Jerry White, *Playboy* Art Director (Courtesy Al Mallette)

Ernie and his Heisman Memorial Trophy, Dec. 6, 1961 (Wide World Photos)

Ernie with President Kennedy in New York after receiving the Heisman Trophy (Courtesy SU Sports Information)

At the Shrine Hospital for Crippled Children in San Francisco prior to annual East- West Shrine game (Courtesy SU Sports Information)

Working out with East team shortly before signing with Cleveland Browns (Courtesy SU Sports Information)

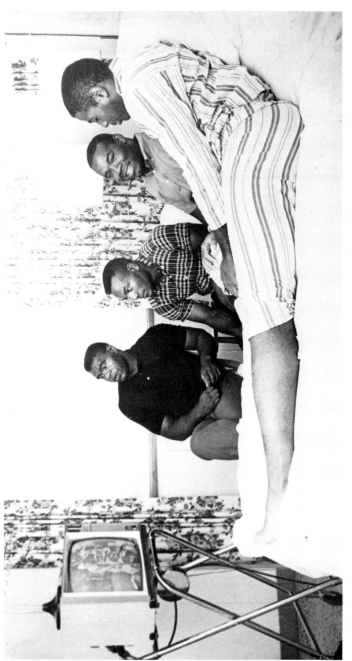

John Wooten, Jim Brown, John Brown and Ernie (left to right) watch the College All-Star game on TV from hospital (Courtesy SU Sports Information)

Art Modell, board chairman of the Cleveland Browns presents Ernie with $15,000 bonus check (Wide World Photos)

Rare publicity photo of Ernie Davis as a Cleveland Brown in 1962 (Courtesy Cleveland Browns)

enough money for their bus fare home. Ernie was unaccountably loyal and protective of the car, however, he responded to the barbs, "This car's alright. It's never broken on me."

John Brown recalled an important occasion when the car did break down on Ernie. During Christmas vacation their junior year, Brown organized a party at his home in Camden, New Jersey. Ernie and Brown drove down in the Edsel. On the way the car's drive shaft broke, and they were stuck for two days. The mechanic had to send to Philadelphia for the part and the instructions on how to install it. Since friends from all over had been invited to the party, Brown's mother had it despite his and Ernie's absence. The two phoned the party and lied about the great time they were having. They had been to the only movie in town, "Moby Dick."

As a result of his banquet, bowl game, and All-Star game appearances, Ernie accrued an impressive collection of trophies, plaques, and watches. Chuck Davis recalled him saying, " 'I got so many watches I'm going to have to give them away.' He finally did too." Periodically, Ernie would arrive home with a box full of awards and deposit them in his closet. His mother would take them out and display them. Today she maintains a part of the collection in her home.

Unlike many celebrities, Ernie never complained about signing autographs. Often when people would thank him for signing, he would thank them for asking. As former teammate Bill Fitzgerald remembered, "He was so well known in the area that he was always recognized. He liked it. He would never turn anybody away because he knew fame was fleeting and was not going to last forever."

In the evenings at the dorm, Ernie would sign publicity photographs for the athletic department, which were then sent out in response to fan requests. One signing was particularly poignant. A nurse asked Fitzgerald if he could get Ernie's autograph. She wanted it for an eight-year-old terminally ill leukemia patient who was a fan of Ernie's.

She thought the autograph might improve his failing spirits.

One night Fitzgerald requested one of the autographed pictures from Ernie, who was amused that his friend wanted an autograph. Fitzgerald told Ernie about the nurse and her request. Touched, Ernie then wrote a personal note on the back of the photo containing the message "never give up." Within months, Ernie was diagnosed as having leukemia.

Prior to attending the Cleveland Browns and the College All-Star summer training camps, Ernie played in the second annual Coaches All-American game in Buffalo, New York. It was extremely hot for Buffalo that week during practice, but the players were loose for their final game before joining pro training camps. For Ernie Davis, it was to be his final game. While in Buffalo, Ernie had some personal articles stolen, sprained his ankle, hurt is calf, and played below his usual standard. During practice, Ernie experienced gum problems and canker sores developed. Teammates John Brown and Bob Ferguson kidded Ernie for "messing with those bad ladies."

At the beginning of the training camp, the East head coach, Woody Hayes of Ohio State, had been admittedly anti-Davis because he won the Heisman Trophy over Ohio State's Bob Ferguson. Syracuse coach Ben Schwartzwalder, an assistant coach for the East recalled, "From the beginning, Ferguson was going to be the star. There weren't even any running plays for Ernie at the start." After observing Ernie at practice, however, Hayes said, "Seeing Ernie daily doing his job, makes his beating out Fergy hurt a lot less."

When he was introduced at the beginning of the game, the hometown Buffalo Bills fans booed Ernie unmercifully for signing with the Cleveland Browns. Ernie did not play particularly well and was used mostly as a blocker and a decoy as quarterback Roman Gabriel and Ferguson led the East to a 13–8 victory.

Expecting more from the Heisman Trophy winner, the

fans booed Ernie's performance. Questioned in the dressing room after the game about his reaction to the booing, Ernie responded, "I've never heard them before, but then, I didn't play too well either." His former high-school coach Marty Harrigan attended the game and recollected, "Ernie didn't feel well and didn't play well. His damper was down. If you are what he is, you expect big things. He didn't have that big a night."

After Ernie's death, a memorial award was established in his honor to be presented annually at the Coaches All-American game. It is awarded to "the player who most impressed his coaches with a general attitude of cooperation, leadership, cheerfulness, and all-round conduct on and off the field." The fans in Buffalo were the originators of the idea for the trophy.

In hindsight, many recall this game as a time when Ernie's later detected illness might have been affecting him. In the locker room, Ernie mentioned to John Brown, "I'm really tired." Brown answered, "It was hot out there tonight and I was kinda tired also." John Mackey attended the game and remembers saying at the time "Somethings wrong with Ernie." Then he dismissed the idea thinking that Woody Hayes must be holding Ernie back to make Bob Ferguson look better.

Ernie and Brown decided to make quick trips home before meeting again at the Cleveland Browns pre-season training camp at Hiram, Ohio. From there, Ernie would depart for the College All-Star camp in Evanston, Illinois, to prepare for the August 3rd game against the NFL champion Green Bay Packers.

Bill Fitzgerald saw Ernie in Elmire prior to his departure for training camp. It was the only time he ever saw Ernie down. "Ernie said, 'I wish I was just going to Ohio, and I wasn't going to Chicago. I'm beat.' "

Marty Harrigan had six children to whom Ernie was very close, and he often stopped by the house to visit. Some of the children and their playmates would tease, "Ernie Davis is no good," and then be delighted when

Ernie chased them around the yard. He stopped by Harrigan's just before leaving for camp. Ernie had a big appetite and usually had something to eat, particularly hot dogs, during his visits. That day he declined everything, including hot dogs because of his bleeding gums. He said he'd have them checked. After he left, the surprised kids said to their father, "Ernie didn't have any hot dogs today, Dad. No hot dogs!"

While eating breakfast one morning his mother noticed the problems Ernie was having with his mouth. She recalled, "He said he was having problems eating and chewing. I told him he had better go to the dentist. He said it didn't seem to be his teeth, but that he would check after he got to camp."

Ernie reported to the Browns camp on July 8th and his oral problems continued. He was diagnosed as having trench mouth and needing two wisdom teeth extracted. As a result of the extractions, Ernie missed the first three days of the All-Star camp. His mouth remained sore and he continued to have problems eating.

Despite the physical problems, Ernie said he felt in good football playing condition. His wind was strong, and he was not tiring as easily as before. In a scrimmage against the Chicago Bears, a week before the All-Star game, Ernie was the leading rusher. Despite the heat and the humidity, Ernie always stayed after practice to sign autographs for all who asked. On Monday, July 30, Ernie awoke with swelling in his neck. A trainer routinely sent him to the hospital in nearby Evanston, Illinois. It was thought to be either mumps or mononucleosis. Ernie was not alarmed and assumed he would play in Friday night's game against the Green Bay Packers.

Leukemia

Throughout the last ten months of Ernie's life, his medical condition fluctuated. On the threshold of attaining his lifelong goal of playing professional football, Ernie Davis was stricken with an illness, referred to only as a "blood disorder." It was, in fact, acute monocytic leukemia. Initially Ernie was told he could not play football for the upcoming season. Then, after two months of treatment, he reached a state of complete remission and the doctor said he could begin playing football. The Cleveland coaching staff however decided not to activate him for the 1962 season. During the off-season, the leukemia returned, and he died three months later.

All of us at one time or another in our lives have experienced the bitter disappointment of a hope unfulfilled, a deserved reward withheld. How natural it is on such occasions to blame fate, to pity oneself. But Ernie held no one responsible. He showed no bitterness or depression. He didn't seek escape or go on a binge. There was uncommon courage. There was the will to keep on trying and the hope that he would overcome his illness. Ernie wanted no sympathy because he felt it wasn't necessary.

Art Modell said, "I was deeply impressed by his great courage. He was totally unselfish. He didn't cry or bemoan his fate. He never once asked, Why me?"

Anyone who didn't know he had terminal leukemia would never have guessed it by observing him. Chuck Davis recalled, "He never talked about his condition." Former teammate Bill Fitzgerald said, "He never mentioned leukemia. He didn't want sympathy. He seemed to have made peace with himself and God. He did not wait idly for death. He never resigned himself to loosing or quitting. He did today what he had done yesterday."

In *Sport* magazine Jim Brown recorded his impressions of Ernie during his illness.

> I knew Ernie when he was perfectly healthy. I knew him when he was sick. I watched him when he was sick. I watched him when I knew he had leukemia but he didn't. I watched him after he found out. I tried to see a difference. There wasn't any. He asked for nothing, wanted no special considerations but was always grateful for whatever he received. And his greatness was that no one ever tried to take advantage of his good heart.
>
> He took his illness on his own shoulders, carried it, lived normally, simply. It was a tremendous thing to watch.

To allay the public's concerns, Ernie consented to write an article for *The Saturday Evening Post* magazine, which he titled, "I'm Not Unlucky." His intention was to show that he had been fortunate enough to accomplish a great deal in a relatively short time. He felt this was the true measure of his life, no matter what the outcome of the leukemia would be. After publicaton of the article six weeks before his death, Ernie was concerned that readers might misunderstand it. Jim Brown wrote that he worried, "that readers might have misinterpreted it as bragging, or as an attempt to say he was something special."

Bob August, a sports writer for the *Cleveland Press* collaborated with Ernie on the article. He wrote at the time of Ernie's death, "I asked him to look through a pile of sports books to see if there might be any he would want. As he shuffled through them, he came to Roy Campanella's book, *It's Good to be Alive*. Davis gave it one of his small, shy smiles. 'I guess I won't be wanting this one,' he said."

His courage inspired family, friends, and fans across the

country. Those who knew him still speak of it 20 years after his death. If Ernie had been no more than a sports figure, he would hardly have inspired this kind of affection. Everyone said that his life had been changed because of Ernie Davis, and more importantly, that they still think of him and draw inspiration from him.

John Brown recalled: "Never once during that period of time did he indicate to me that he had given up hope, and that is the one thing that has stuck with me to this day. I tell my kids that over and over again. He knew he was dying, but he always said to me that just because he was dying didn't mean he had to give up trying. I've always kept that in the back of my mind." Brown told an anecdote illustrating Ernie's concern for others even during his illness. As a new young lineman in the NFL, Brown was having trouble mastering the techniques of pass blocking, an art that was not stressed at Syracuse University, a reknowned running team. He recalled his frustration over mastering the techniques. "I came home from practice, and was complaining about how tough pass blocking was. I was down." Ernie said, 'You may not make it, but you don't have to give up trying.' Here I was complaining about a football game. He's talking about life and not giving up trying."

During Ernie's illness, he and fullback Jim Brown developed a close association. After Ernie died, Brown wrote:

I've always felt that words, great and courage have been overused and abused. I have never been one to take them idly. I say with the utmost sincerity: Ernie Davis, to me, was the greatest, most courageous person I have ever met. He made our lives better, brighter and fuller because we were privileged to know him.

The symptoms of Ernie's fatal illness first became evident during the College All-Stars training camp in July, 1962 at the Northwestern University campus in Evanston, Illinois. Shortly after his arrival, Ernie spent one day in the hospital to stop bleeding from extraction of two wisdom teeth. Over the last weekend in July, the glands in his neck became swollen. Although he felt fine, as a precaution the East trainer sent him to the hospital on Monday, July 30. It was assumed he had mumps or mononucleosis and would still be able to participate in the game against the world champion Green Bay Packers on Friday.

The routine blood tests performed at the hospital immediately revealed the seriousness of Ernie's condition. The doctors took bone marrow scrappings from his chest. The samples confirmed leukemia. At the time, Ernie and the public were told only that he had a "blood disorder." The doctors surmised that Ernie was probably initially afflicted in April 1962.

Leukemia is a cancer of the blood forming tissues in the body, the bone marrow, the lymph nodes, and the spleen. In leukemia, abnormal white cells invade these tissues inducing swelling. Ernie was stricken with acute monocytic leukemia, the rarest form, accounting for less than 5 percent of all leukemia cases. It is characterized by the production of an extremely high number of abnormal white blood cells called monocytes.

The function of normal white blood cells is to fight infections by destroying bacteria, viruses, and foreign matter in the blood and help build immunity to disease. With the normal white blood cells unable to function properly, infections occur repeatedly. With the increased production of abnormal white cells, the production of red blood cells which carry oxygen to all parts of the body decreases, causing anemia. Platelet production, essential for the clotting of blood, is also reduced, resulting in excessive bleeding, bruising and hemorrhaging.

The College All-Stars were coached by former Cleveland Browns star Otto Graham, who noted that Ernie did not perform well during practice sessions. The coach said, "Some of the kids who played against him say he's much better than he has shown here and this thing may have been coming on." According to Graham, however, Ernie had not performed well enough to be a starter. Nevertheless, in a scrimmage against the Chicago Bears a week before the All Star game, Ernie had been the most productive back as he gained 17 yards on three carries and 21 yards on two pass receptions. Long after the scrimmage ended, Ernie remained signing autographs on the hot humid afternoon. He was the last player to leave the field. *Chicago Tribune* sports reporter David Condon wrote, "Ernie left lots of happy youngsters, boys and girls, a few nuns, and hard-bitten football fans in his wake as he inched toward the dressing room."

When he checked into the hospital, Ernie said, "The swelling has gone down some. It started yesterday, but was worse this morning. I had a fever, but not a very high one when I checked into the hospital. They have been running some tests here, but they haven't told me a thing." Dr. Franklin Kaiser was the attending physician at Evanston General Hospital and he ruled out the initial reports Ernie was suffering from mumps or mono. He said, "I haven't come to any conclusions. I won't know until further tests are made. I realize people in Cleveland are anxious to know about Ernie, but I don't have any more information right now." Asked if Ernie's career would be affected, the doctor said he couldn't answer that question.

Art Modell flew to Evanston on Wednesday morning, August 1, to get a first-hand report on Ernie's condition. "I'm hoping for the best," he said. "Ernie's undergoing a series of tests. I'm going up there to make sure he has the best of everything. Depending on what I learn today, Ernie may be moved to Mayo or Cleveland Clinic. It seems to be a blood disorder. Our only thought is to get Ernie well." On the same day, Tony DeFilippo flew in from Elmira and spent most of the evening with Ernie.

While visiting Ernie in the hospital on Wednesday, Modell pulled no punches in describing the situation. Because of his illness, Ernie would not be able to play in the College All-Star game.

Since he didn't feel sick, Ernie was shaken by the news that he could not play football. Modell said, "This is a very sick boy and he cried when I visited him this afternoon. This boy means more at this moment than the entire football season. We will see him through to the last down."

Ernie's tears were of disappointment and it was to be his only public emotional display of his illness. As Ernie said, "It was the first big game he had missed in 13 years."

Modell announced plans to fly Ernie from Evanston to Cleveland on Friday, "for a thorough analysis." When informed of the travel plans, Ernie said to Modell, "I haven't got a hurt in me. Why don't they let me go?" He arrived in Cleveland around noon accompanied by Modell and Marsh Samuel, the Browns publicity director. Ernie walked off the plane without difficulty and appeared in good spirits when he stopped to talk with reporters. "The doctors haven't told me anything yet about my condition," Ernie said. Modell immediately jumped in and said, "Tests on Ernie's condition are not complete by any means. That is why he's going to Marymount Hospital." To those who saw him, Ernie appeared to still have swelling on the left side of his neck. The news that Ernie would not play in the All-Star game was the first indication of the gravity of Ernie's condition. John Brown said, "That's rough. Ernie really wanted to play in that game and show something. I don't recall anything ever being wrong with him at Syracuse." The Browns coach Paul Brown, said his first reaction to the news "was deep dejection and discouragement. It was hard to make myself believe that Ernie's case was really as serious as it now appears. If he's out any length of time, this could be a crusher. We have high hopes for Ernie."

Coach Brown gave John Brown, Jim Brown, and John Wooten Friday night off so they could watch the All-Star game with Ernie in the hospital. On seeing them, Ernie kidded Jim Brown about loosing a sprint in training camp to rookie Sam Tidmore. He told them, "I haven't felt sick yet." Jim Brown wrote of the evening, "Not once did he talk about himself or his disappointment. Instead he told us about players on the All-Star team, how big they were and their abilities.

The NFL champion Packers, 23-point favorites, scored three touchdowns in the fourth quarter to rout the All-Stars 42-20. Green Bay quarterback Bart Starr passed for five touchdowns and 255 yards. In an unusual display of sportsmanship, the winners inspired by their captain, Jim Ringo, a former Syracuse University player, voted the game ball to Ernie. All-Star Coach Otto Graham said in the locker room after the game, "We missed Davis. . .I have a lot of respect for the Packers. They're a high class outfit. They voted to give the game ball to Ernie Davis." Jim Brown wrote, "He was obviously touched when it was announced that the Packers had voted to award him the game ball."

Although there had been no public announcement of the extent of Ernie's illness, some reporters began to wonder. Frank Gibbons of the *Cleveland Press* wrote, "Obviously, his doctors do not feel that his condition is good because they gave him up to Modell and further analysis in Cleveland." Columnist Red Smith wrote of the game ball presentation by the Packers, ". . .that set some guys wondering. And pretty soon the truth was around the sports beat, though it was much later before there was a public announcement."

In Cleveland, Dr. Austin Weisberger, a noted hematologist, became Ernie's personal physician. Tony DeFilippo brought an Elmira internist, Dr. Gerald P. Schneider, with him to Cleveland as a medical advisor. "I knew nothing about leukemia," the lawyer said in a recent interview. "Dr. Schneider came to Cleveland as a favor to me. I wanted him to find out what this was about. I didn't know Dr. Weisberger or any of those doctors."

On arrival in Cleveland, they went to the Brown's offices and met with Art Modell and Dr. Vic Ippolito, the Browns' team doctor. At this time, Ernie still had not been told the diagnosis of his illness. Dr. Ippolito was in favor of telling Ernie he had leukemia while DeFilippo was adamantly opposed. "No way," he said. "You can't tell a guy as sick as he is that he's got leukemia, that he's going to die. I disagree with you." They continued to argue and disagree. Without resolving the question they departed for the hospital.

Dr. Weisberger permitted Dr. Schneider to look at all the

slides and records. DeFilippo remembered, "When Dr. Schneider came back to me, he was sweating. He said, 'Tony, he's got it.' " They then had a meeting in Dr. Weisberger's office. Recalled DeFilippo, Dr. Weisberger said, "Gentlemen, we have a paramedical problem here. Should Ernie and the public know? It's my considered opinion he should not know." That ended the discussion. One reason Dr. Weisberger gave for not telling Ernie the severity of his condition was that he first wanted to test Ernie's reaction to the drugs he was being treated with.

To allay growing press speculation, the Cleveland Browns on August 9th held an off-the-record press conference. For the first time they announced that Ernie's "blood disorder" was leukemia. They said he had 6-12 months to live. The Browns emphasized Ernie had not been informed, consequently it was imperative that silence be maintained. Val Pinchbeck, former Syracuse University Sports Information Director, recalled how he was informed. "Arnie Burdick, the sports editor of the *Syracuse Herald-Journal*, went to Cleveland. Later, I was at a party and Arnie arrived. I waved. The people between us parted. He's as white as a ghost coming at me. He grabbed me aside and said, 'Ernie.' I said, 'What?' He said, "He's got leukemia. He's got about six months to live."

Elmira sportswriter Al Mallette will never forget how he first learned of the seriousness of Ernie's illness. He was the official scorer at a baseball game at Dunn Field in August 1962, when Tony DeFilippo called him in the pressbox from Chicago. "Tony said, 'Al, Ernie's all done.' At first I thought he just meant for the College All-Star game. He said, 'It's a sad story. He's got leukemia,' I was in shock for the rest of the game."

Mrs. Radford, Ernie's mother, traveled to Cleveland on August 11th and demanded to be told the complete truth about Ernie's "blood disorder." Since it was a weekend, she could not reach Dr. Weisberger so she contacted Dr. Ippolito of the Browns and made an appointment to see him immediately. She recollected: "He could see that I was desperate." I said, 'I want you to tell me. I don't care what it is. It's been so long and they keep saying it's a rare disease.' " The doctor told her he thought she knew. After he told her, Mrs. Radford kept the secret to herself and her husband.

Syracuse University coaches Ben Schwartzwalder, Rocco Pirro, Ted Dailey, and Bill Bell went to visit Ernie in the hospital in Cleveland. Schwartzwalder recalled,

> Before we went in the room, a nurse said, "This will be the last time you'll ever see him." We didn't know what his status was until we got to the hospital. We went in to see him and we think, "This is it." We stayed and stayed. We got up to go after three hours and Ernie placed himself in the doorway. He said, "Please don't go. This will be the last time I'll ever see you." That didn't sound like somebody who thought he was going to live. He must have known then. He wasn't depressed. He just wanted us to talk some more and we did. Finally we left. We got in the hall and we all just cried like babies. You know he never talked about himself. We just talked about football things."

John Mackey also visited Ernie at the hospital in mid-August. Throughout their Syracuse careers the two roommates often good naturedly teased one another about which of them was the better football player. Mackey recalled, "When I visited the hospital the first thing Ernie said was, 'I'm going to play next year and we'll find out which one of us is best.' I said, 'We sure will.'"

Ernie spent approximately three weeks in the hospital, but was not bed ridden. He even attended some practices at the Browns training camp in Hiram, Ohio. While in the hospital he also studied the team's playbook. He said, "All I can do is hope and pray I'll be back. I hope I don't waste too much time." On August 18th, Ernie attended the first pro football doubleheader, a new concept of Art Modell's. The pre-season games matched the Dallas Cowboys against the Detroit Lions and the Browns against the Pittsburgh Steelers.

Unknown to anyone but Modell and the public address announcer, Ernie was introduced as the 12th member of the Browns offensive team at the start of the game. He walked across the field in the spotlight as 77,683 fans gave him a sustained five-minute standing ovation. Modell recalled, "It was not unlike Lou Gehrig's farewell at Yankee Stadium. It was an overwhelming tribute to Ernie from the fans. It was the last time, it was the only time he was on the playing field for the Cleveland Browns."

Another who had vivid memories was John Brown, "I'll never forget that night when he walked out. That spotlight hit him, and those people just went wild. He walked from the dugout to where the pitcher's mound would be. Everybody fell in love with Ernie Davis in Cleveland." It was, Brown thought, because "he exuded class. He was always smiling." That evening when they returned to their apartment and discussed the event, Brown said, "Ernie just shook his head. He could not believe the people would give him that kind of ovation."

In addition to the fans, Ernie also won the hearts of many of his teammates. That night veteran lineman and placekicking star Lou Groza brought his three sons into the locker room. "This is Ernie Davis, Jeff," he said to one of his sons. "Isn't he a good looking fellow?" Jeff thrust a program at Ernie and said softly, "Can I have your autograph?" Ernie quickly complied.

With Dr. Weisberger's consent, Tony DeFilippo took Ernie to the National Institute of Health in Bethesda, Maryland on August 22. The purpose of the trip was to get additional medical opinions on Ernie's condition. Word of his arrival had reached the press so they entered through a rear door. Dr.Berlin, head of cancer research, personally supervised Ernie's case. Dr. Berlin assured DeFilippo that everything that was medically possible was being done for Ernie by Dr. Weisberger. The key to the treatment was chemotherapy with the drug six mercaptopurine (MP-6). After a couple of days, Ernie was released from the hospital and returned to Elmira for a vacation. Even while his career was shrouded in uncertainty, Ernie continued to demonstrate his lifelong concern for others. While at NIH he sent a personal letter of thanks to the nurses who had cared for him at Marymount Hospital in Cleveland.

Since he felt and looked fine the hospitalization and the medical tests seemed unnecessary to him. Never one to be idle, the inactivity of his hospital stay was a burden. In *The Saturday Evening Post* he wrote, "What I remember most from last summer is waking up early in the morning and staring at the hospital walls. There was nothing to do except think. At first, that was the worst part of it. It was a very lonely time."

Ernie probably inferred the gravity of his condition through conversations, letters, and the endless medical tests, although he never specifically stated that he knew. In the magazine article he wrote, "During all that time I didn't press the doctors to tell me what was wrong. Even now I am not sure why I didn't. The little things I heard people say, the uncertainties, were hard to live with. At the same time, down deep inside, I was afraid of what the answer would be. So I put off asking the question."

Without having to ask the question, Ernie received the answer on October 4th. That day Dr. Weisberger asked Ernie to drop by his office. When he arrived, Art Modell and Dr. Ippolito were already there. After some initial small talk, Dr. Weisberger told Ernie they were going to inform him of his condition. The doctor began by noting Ernie's excellent physical well-being and how well he responded to treatment. Then for the first time Ernie heard the word leukemia. In the magazine article, he wrote of his reaction. "It's a word that jumps out at you, a frightening word. I can't imagine what my reaction would have been if they had told me my first few days in the hospital. Now there was only the first shock, and that was all. For a long time I realized leukemia was one of the possibilities."

Ernie was told that the treatment had been effective, that all traces of leukemia had left his body, and that he now had an adequate supply of white cells, red cells and platelets. Contrary to a widespread belief, remission is not part of the normal course of leukemia. It is also not the same as a cure.

Initially Ernie was reluctant to have the nature of his illness publicized, but he finally agreed to a carefully worded statement. The statement read in part; ". . .Davis has had a form of leukemia. He has responded well to therapy and medication. At the present time his blood findings are entirely normal. As long as he remains in this perfect state of remission, I see no reason why he can't play professional football."

Ernie wrote of his reaction to the news;

> . . .now I knew what I was battling and that there was some-
> thing to look forward to—football. Some place along the line
> you have to come to an understanding with yourself, and I had
> reached mine a long time before, when I was still in the hospi-
> tal. Either you fight or you give up. For a time I was so
> despondent I would just lie there, not even wanting to move.
> One day I got hold of myself. I decided I would face up to what
> I had and try to beat it. I still feel that way.

Shortly afterward, Ernie met with reporters and he seemed in fine spirits as he talked about his future. Asked if he was upset by the news of his illness, Ernie said, "No. The doctor told me man to man. I didn't know what I had, but I knew it must be serious. I already had made up my mind to accept it and live with it, whatever it was. I'm 100 per cent now and hoping to stay that way."

After Ernie died, Jim Brown talked to Dr. Weisberger, and wrote this account of the October 4th meeting. "Ernie's first reaction was: Can I lick it? The doctor replied that people were known to live normal lives for a long time with it. Ernie perspired a little and remained quiet. Dr. Weisberger told me, 'I don't believe for a minute that he wasn't upset but he never showed it. Not once.' "

At the press conference, it was brought out that the remission was the result of traditional medication and not experimental drugs. Art Modell said, "This has happened before in other cases. You can't call it a miracle. It's remarkable though. There are no traces of the illness." In describing the meeting with Dr. Weisberger, Modell recalled, "Ernie conveyed a sense almost of exhilaration when he was told he could begin working out. He had been mystified by rumors that he had all sorts of ailments. "

Later Dr. Weisberger told Brown the remission was "semi-miraculous." Brown wrote, "He explained it's not uncommon for adults to become remissive but the completeness of Ernie's, he said, was remarkable." How long the temporary state would last was a matter of speculation.

With the opportunity to play football once again a possiblity and with the worst seemingly behind him, Ernie eagerly began his conditioning workouts on October 8th. The team physician, Dr. Ippolito, supervised a program of calisthenics, jogging, and wind sprints aimed at getting Ernie ready to play.

While his teammates prepared for each week's game, Ernie worked to join them. Eleven games remained on the Browns schedule and Ernie's goal was to be ready for some of them. "I'm enjoying myself a lot now," he said. "It's like living a normal life again. . .if you have too much time to think you go crazy—I mean the worrying about things."

The fans, as usual, supported Ernie. He received hundreds of letters of encouragement which he answered. "The people all over the country have been wonderful to me," he said. "I want to thank them." One of the most amazing aspects of Ernie's career was the respect opposing team's fans always showed him. Two weeks after the public announcement of his leukemia, Ernie sat on the Syracuse bench at Beaver Stadium on the Penn State University campus. The Orangemen and the Nittany Lions were archrivals. It was announced to the crowd that Ernie was on the bench. The 47,000 fans in attendance responded with a standing ovation. Forever shunning the limelight, Ernie remained seated until the P.A. announcer prodded, "Ernie, will you take a bow." He stood shyly and nodded to the crowd.

However, not everyone was as pleased as Ernie and the fans about his return to football. There were some concerns expressed by members of the medical community about the wisdom of Ernie's return to playing. The controversy has continued on and off to the present day.

The dissenting doctors seemed mostly concerned that Ernie's case might give false hopes to other leukemia patients, their families, and their friends. Dr. George A. Resta, who treated the Washington Redskins and the

Washington Senators, said, "I am not familiar with the facts of the case, but if Davis has true leukemia, I certainly wouldn't advise that he resume his duties as a professional football player. It is not good for other leukemia patients to read this sort of thing haphazardly. They might try to do strenuous things themselves and it might prove fatal."

Dr. James Grace, a researcher and clinician at Roswell Park Memorial Hospital in Buffalo was quoted by the wire services as saying, "I doubt very seriously that he (Davis) would be 100 per cent, and I doubt it would be fair to his teammates or even to opposing players, let alone to him." Although the doctor felt patients in remission should live as normally as possible, he added, "But this is different. This is hard tough football. The more I think of it, the more ridiculous it seems."

Dr. Sidney Farber of Boston's Children's Hospital took a more moderate position. "How much rough and tumble can be taken is a question. We don't advise fisticuffs or football for our patients in remission, but I suppose if I had leukemia, I would try to live life to the hilt."

Questioned on the issue, Modell pointed out that, "all those who are against Ernie playing haven't examined him. The specialists we have consulted—and I have the utmost confidence in their ability—say after examining him completely, that in his present condition, having the disease does not heighten his chance of injury." The question became moot, however, when Cleveland coach Paul Brown refused to activate Ernie during the 1962 season.

A close personal relationship developed between Ernie and Art Modell, which is a tribute to both men. On the surface, Ernie was an employee, but Modell began to take a personal interest in him during their contract negotiations. When Ernie was stricken, Modell reacted as a friend. Ernie's well being became his primary objective. During his illness the Cleveland Browns paid Ernie's salary and medical expenses at a cost of approximately $10,000. Although Modell had an investment in Ernie, morally he wasn't obligated to go as far as he did in obtaining medical opinions.

Ernie was examined by 13 specialists in five institutions.

Modell explained, "He was determined to beat it. That's why I gave him every chance to do it. I took him around the country for examinations and tests. I was deeply impressed by his courage. The only thing he complained about is how much it was costing me."

"Art spent a lot of time and money trying to get opinions for Ernie's disease," said John Brown. "Even though you have an investment there, if Dr. Weisberger, who was an authority, tells you something, you leave it there. When you continue further, then I think that's out of love to help that other person."

All of Ernie's friends speak glowingly of the treatment he received from Art Modell. John Brown said, "Art developed a real fatherly love for Ernie as he got to know him and know what kind of person he was. He really did. I think he really took care of Ernie during that period of time. Ernie never had one negative thing to say about Art. It was always praise about Art."

Tony DeFilippo said, "Art Modell was wonderful to Ernie. The proof of the pudding to see who was really concerned about Ernie Davis occurred at his funeral. Art Modell chartered a plane so the Cleveland Browns players and officials could attend the funeral."

In his autobiography, *Off My Chest*, Jim Brown wrote,

> I imagine you have to know Art to be as certain as I am that his concern for Ernie had nothing whatever to do with the fact that Ernie represented a small fortune gone down the drain. Having given up Bobby Mitchell and a first round draft choice for the right to hand Ernie an eighty-thousand-dollar contract, Art's total loss amounted to hundreds of thousands in player property value. That kind of money carries a lot of meaning to Art because he came into his money the hard way, starting as an electrician's helper at eighty-seven cents an hour. Yet more than anything else, Art is a compassionate man. He had grown fond of Ernie during the time they'd negotiated a contract, and now, hang the cost, Art was going to do everything possible to make Ernie's last months as pleasant as possible.

John Brown was soliciting funds in 1979 for Syracuse

University's Ernie Davis Memorial Room in the brand new Carrier Dome Stadium. After not having talked to Modell in eight years, Brown called him. Without hesitation, Modell pledged a check for $1,000. "He had a distinct fondness for Ernie," Brown said. "He never went to Syracuse University, so he didn't have to do it, but it was for Ernie."

For years on the wall in his office Modell had a large picture of Ernie Davis standing on the field in a Browns uniform. Today, he says simply of his friendship with Ernie, "We had a close relationship. I was a surrogate father who adopted him. I never met anyone like him before or since."

There was only one dissenter in the praise for Modell. In 1979, Coach Paul Brown published his autobiography, *PB: The Paul Brown Story,* in which he gave his opinion about the controversy about whether or not Ernie should have been permitted to play professional football. He wrote critically of Modell's motives and vigorously defended his own. After the 1962 season, when Modell fired Brown, for whom the Cleveland Browns were named, many felt the controversy about Ernie was a contributing factor.

Coach Brown had a reason for not activating Ernie during the 1962 professional football season. Dr. James Hewlett, his neighbor, was a hematologist and helped conduct blood tests on Ernie at the Cleveland Clinic. Brown asked Dr. Hewlett if Ernie should play with leukemia. According to the coach, Dr. Hewlett advised against it. As a result, Brown decided not to play Ernie.

Brown, now part-owner and general manager of the Cincinnati Bengals, was critical of Modell for cultivating the impression that Ernie might play during the 1962 season, when Brown had already decided that wouldn't happen based on Dr. Hewlett's recommendation. Brown wrote, "Next we were told Ernie 'had recovered' and could play; that was deliberately misleading and built up only more false hopes."

Brown's sharpest and probably most unfair criticism of Modell was the allegation that Modell wanted to play Ernie to recoup part of his financial investment. Brown wrote: "Finally Modell came to me and said, 'Put him in the game and let him play. We have a large investment in him and I'd like a chance to get some of it back. It doesn't matter how long he plays. Just let him run back a kick. Let him do anything, so we can get a story in the paper saying he's going to play and the fans will come to see him. If he has to go, why not let him have a little fun.' . . . "

Brown contended that he then contacted NFL Commissioner Pete Rozelle saying, "I'm getting a lot of heat to activate and play Ernie Davis for a short time for publicity purposes. I don't want to do it, but I think you should know about the situation."

According to Brown, Rozelle responded, "Don't activate him. If you do, I'll step into this matter and overrule you, and I don't want to get involved."

"Thus my decision stood," wrote Brown, "but from that time forward, the Paul Brown-Art Modell relationship really went into the deep freeze."

Brown summarized,

> The entire situation was unfair to Ernie, of course, whom I liked very much because he was such a pleasant and courageous person. He never once asked me if he could practice or play, but I'm sure all the needless publicity about his chances had to upset him. I know it upset our players and haunted us throughout that season. Our players saw him nearly every day at practice, where he'd don a sweatsuit, but do little more than warm up the quarterbacks or run laps. He was so ill the sweat just poured from him even as he stood watching us work. That frightened and unnerved many of our guys, who had never before watched a man in this condition. Sometimes, when we walked onto the practice field, they looked at him, and everything got very quiet. It became just heartbreaking.

Modell filed a grievance with the NFL claiming that Brown's book constituted violation of the league by-law prohibiting a member of one club from publically criticizing another club or its members. Brown was fined $10,000 by NFL Commissioner Pete Rozelle for violating that rule. At a news conference, Brown said he did not intend to hurt or embarrass anyone, but he "stands on facts."

The two antagonists' versions of what happened are probably not as different as they appear on the surface. Modell, aware of Ernie's intense desire to appear in a Cleveland uniform, may well have put some pressure on the coach to let him play briefly. Brown, disposed to put the worst possible construction on Modell's motivations, may well have misinterpreted the pressure.

Probably the best summary of the controversy was offered by Dr. Vic Ippolito, the Browns team doctor for 32 years and still a consultant to the team. He stated at a press conference after publication of Paul Brown's book, "I was the one who had the final decision whether Ernie Davis should play, and although Dr. Weisberger said he could play, I had the final say and I agreed with him. Nobody, including Art Modell, could tell me who could and couldn't play because of an injury or illness. If it came to that, I would quit right on the spot." Dr. Ippolito had to be convinced Ernie could play because his professional reputation was also at stake if something had happened to Ernie while playing football. At the time of the publication of Brown's autobiography, Dr. Weisberger was deceased.

Dr. Ippolito felt that the relationship that had developed between Ernie and Modell prompted the latter to push for Ernie's being allowed to play once the doctors okayed it. The doctor said, "Art didn't want him to play because of money; he cared about him. He wanted to make an appearance because of the young man. He wanted him to play because Ernie wanted to play football and he knew he was going to die."

Frank Gibbons of the *Cleveland Press* wrote after Ernie's death, "I was among a minority who wanted Ernie to play last year with the Browns, because this was his last chance and he wanted it so badly." The biggest fear was that an injury and a relapse might occur simultaneously. For this and for other reasons many, including Pete Rozelle, were opposed. "Ex-coach Paul Brown can't be blamed for not playing him," wrote Gibbons. "President Art Modell can't be blamed for wanting him played, and I say that because I know Ernie's happiness in the time he had left was his motive. Now I'm glad he didn't play. After all, it's a tough league and he might not have done as well as he would have liked. He might not have done well at all through no fault of his own. That would have made his last winter and his last spring even worse than they must have been."

Ernie wanted to play football with all his heart. If he could have scrimmaged he was certain he could have persuaded the coaches with his performance. He felt he was at his peak level of ability. He said, "This is when it really gets frustrating. I'm in good shape, but it's too late in the season to work me into the setup."

He refused to criticize or confront Coach Brown. The coach, he believed, had to be concerned with the other players on the team and not just with him. John Brown said, "Ernie never knocked Paul Brown. He was a very mature person." According to Jim Brown, the Cleveland players were pleased when the coach was fired. He wrote, "But Ernie Davis, the man who suffered the most, the man who wanted to play pro football more deeply than any of us—if only for a token quarter to see his dream come true—said only: "From the little I know of Paul Brown, I think he is a fine gentleman." Brown noted that even in private conversations, "he always spoke respectfully about the coach."

So for the first time in his life since he began playing organized football in the Small Fry League in Elmira, Ernie was on the sidelines watching rather than playing the 1962 season. During home games, he sat on the bench in street clothes encouraging his teammates and analyzing the opponents. His analytical ability impressed the coaches and the players. Wrote Jim Brown, "It was amazing to me that in a relatively short time he knew as much about the defense of the other team as I knew. He studied the game thoroughly. I'd say, 'What do you think of so and so as a linebacker?' He'd give me a complete analysis which often helped me. He was absorbed in football."

During this time, Ernie and John Brown, two young

bachelors, shared an apartment on East 142nd Street in Cleveland. Teammate Charley Scales, whose wife and children lived in Pittsburgh, slept on the sofa during the football season. When the young players first rented the apartment, Ernie told Art Modell about the great deal he was getting on second-hand furniture. Modell said, "You are a Cleveland Brown now and Cleveland Browns always go first class." So Ernie used part of his bonus money to buy new furniture. None of them were gourmet cooks, but fortunately a woman neighbor would occasionally provided them with a well-cooked meal.

While they were living in Cleveland, Ernie's girlfriend from Syracuse University visited. John Brown was going with a girl from Cleveland and Ernie's girlfriend stayed at her parent's house. Brown fondly recalled that the two couples spent enjoyable evenings together dining and dancing.

Another visitor to the Cleveland apartment was Chuck Davis. While visiting, he chided Ernie, "What are you going to do with all your money?" Ernie mentioned that one thing he had to do was buy his mother a birthday present. With plenty of encouragement from Chuck, he purchased a white Plymouth for his mother's birthday gift. Back in Elmira, they parked the car in front of her house. When she came home from work she inquired about the car. Chuck pretended it was his, but she was skeptical. Finally Ernie ended the suspense by giving her the keys, which came as a complete surprise.

Ernie lived as he always had and made no concessions to his illness. John Brown recalled the response Ernie always received from the children in the neighborhood. "Whenever Ernie and I would walk around," said Brown. "All of a sudden you'd hear a 'Hey there's Ernie Davis,' and we'd be swamped with kids all wanting to talk to Ernie. He loved every second of it."

The Browns did not practice on Monday and Tuesday so the black players and some former black players like Marion Motley would meet at the Carter Hotel in Cleveland.

On Mondays they started playing basketball and Ernie eagerly participated. After seeing him in action, many felt he could have played professionally. Since they had never played football with Ernie, basketball gave some of the players, particularly Jim Brown, an opportunity to see if Ernie measured up.

Brown and Bobby Mitchell had been roommates and were close friends. Initially, when the Davis-Mitchell trade was announced, Brown was uncertain. He knew Mitchell to be an outstanding back, and since he had never played football with Ernie he was unsure of his ability. Brown, a former basketball player at Syracuse found out what type of athletic ability Ernie had while playing basketball with him. Brown wrote, "On the basketball floor I found out this man would have been all he was cracked up to be. Ernie was like a tiger on the floor. He never let up. The way he fought I knew I didn't have to look at him in a football uniform to realize what he might have been. I've thought about it often. He could have contributed so much."

In the off-season, Ernie worked along with Jim Brown, as a sales representative for the Pepsi Cola Company. He also played on the Cleveland Browns basketball team. In his autobiography *Off My Chest,* Jim Brown wrote, "There was hope after the season that he would make it. He ran longer and harder than the rest. He bowled and played golf. He played like a tiger with the basketball team."

In February, Ernie suffered a medical setback: the remission left. Tony DeFilippo went to Cleveland for a visit. Even at that critical time, Ernie remained himself. DeFilippo recalled, "Ernie and I never talked about leukemia up to the day he died. He never tried to burden anybody else with anything. There were no psychological effects. No way. He was a helluva kid."

Dr. Weisberger told Jim Brown, "Ernie's only reaction to the news was 'darn.' " Brown quoted the doctor as saying, "That was the only complaint, literally and truly, that Ernie ever made in all the times I saw him. Not once was a tranquilizer needed. The doctor said Ernie's refusal to complain made it necessary to evaluate his condition by examination of the blood rather than the symptoms Ernie might relate. He always told the doctor, 'I feel fine. I feel strong.' He didn't want to be a bother to us."

The treatment Ernie underwent included regular blood transfusions. Because of his great personal pride and his desire not to burden people with his problems, he tried to conceal the fact that he was receiving transfusions. John Brown remembered, "Ernie would call and say, 'John, I have to go into the hospital today. If anybody calls, tell them I'm out of town.' "

One of the obvious symptoms of leukemia is excessive bleeding caused by the reduced number of platelets in the blood which aid in coagulating. John Brown recalled, "The saddest thing about it was during the last stages of the disease he would bleed a lot. It was almost comical in a way. He'd cut himself shaving and bleed a lot. You could hear him in the bathroom trying to clean up so nobody would see."

Jim Brown wrote of an incident that occured in the spring which left an indelible impression on him. He had driven over to Ernie's apartment to pick him up for a party. "He looked terribly tired," wrote Brown.

> I wanted to say, "Look Ernie, if you're a little tired or you feel under the weather, why not skip the party." I wanted to back out of the party, but I knew if I did Ernie would know why. If I had so much as mentioned that he looked tired, it would have been like hitting him in the belly.
>
> We sat there and talked awhile, all the time I hoped he'd say, I'm a little bushed tonight, Jim. I think I'll skip the party. But of course he didn't say anything of the kind. While we talked, I noticed, suddenly, that Ernie had a small wad of cotton stuffed in his nose. He had stuffed it well up where it could not easily be seen, but it slipped down. Ernie's hand leaped to his face. He pretended to be idly fingering his nose while he stuffed the cotton back into place. I looked the other way pretending not to notice. I was sick at heart. Nose bleeds, I knew, were a grave sign. The speck of blood told me it was the beginning of the end.

Journey's End

In the two weeks preceeding his death, Ernie visited Syracuse and Elmira. It was a farewell, but only he realized it. His condition was well known, but it was easy to avoid thinking about. Ernie went out of his way during his visits to project a confident attitude, even stating that he was looking forward to playing football in the fall. Ernie's death on Saturday, May 18, 1963 was both expected and unexpected by his friends. As John Mackey said, "He didn't look or act sick, so we believed what he told us." The occasion for Ernie's visit to Syracuse was to act as assistant coach in the annual spring Alumni-Varsity football game. Coach Ben Schwartzwalder recalled, "He was enthusiastic. Full of fire and vigor. It didn't dampen his spirits any. I can see him now over on the alumni bench cheering and yelling." Many did not notice any physical difference in him. He had lost some weight, but he wore a vest to conceal it. During the game, Walt Sweeney of the alumni, soon to become a star guard in the NFL, was ejected for fighting. Ernie ran onto the field and argued with the officials that Sweeney should be out "for just one play." Incredibly they agreed, a tribute no doubt to Ernie's popularity. Among those who saw Ernie in Syracuse was John Mackey. After Ernie's death he said, "I talked to him when he was up here for the alumni game. He looked like he had lost some weight, but he was in good spirits. He said if he continued to feel as good as he did then, he'd be back playing ball again this fall." Professional lineman Maury Youmans, a teammate on the 1959 National Championship squad, coached with Ernie that day. "He could hardly wait to begin playing with the Cleveland Browns," Youmans recalled. "He looked in excellent shape. . ."

Before returning to Cleveland, Ernie stopped off in Elmira for his last visit home. As usual he visited Marty Harrigan and his family. The high school coach remembered, "He was in good spirits and looked fine. He told me all about the game." After Ernie's death, Mrs. Harrigan said, "He stopped in recently and spent an hour and a half playing games and rolling around with the children. And when word gets around he's here, all the kids in the neighborhood flock to the house for a look."

Back in Cleveland, Ernie still betrayed no sign of a decline in his condition. As he always had on the athletic field, Ernie ran with his head up until the end. He traveled around Ohio representing the soft drink company and he analyzed opponents' game films for the Browns. His film work was considered to be of coach's quality and was a great help to the team during the 1963 season. He bowled and had just purchased a new set of golf clubs. He had been a caddy as a child and was now becoming a good golfer. To everyone, Ernie talked positively of the future. He was excited about buying a new car. He also continued to be an avid reader. Just before entering the hospital, he finished *The Ugly American*, which he recommended to John Brown.

On the afternoon of Thursday, May l6th, Ernie checked into the hospital for the final time. That morning was the last time John Brown saw Ernie and later he could not recall anything unusual occurring. Brown said, "Never once did I detect a weakening in Ernie, mentally or physically. He was just the same old Ern, never thinking about himself, just content with being one of the guys." Returning to their apartment that afternoon, Brown found a note from Ernie which read, "Going to the hospital for a few days. Don't tell anybody. I'll see you around."

Prior to checking into the hospital, Ernie stopped by the Browns' offices to see Art Modell. He apologized for the cost of his medical care. He also talked of the future, expressing the belief that the Browns would win the National Football League Championship for the coming season. In recalling the scene shortly afterward, Modell realized that normally Ernie called before coming to see him. "He was here for one hour," Modell said. "He told me he had to go to the hospital, but that it was nothing serious and that he would be out of there in a couple of days. His neck was swollen considerably and we all knew what it meant. I think Ernie did too. He was coming by to say good bye to me and the others. I asked him how he was feeling. All he would say was that I've felt better, but it's nothing to worry about. My throat hurts a little. He was apologetic about having to go in the hospital."

With his characteristic concern not to upset anyone, Ernie didn't even notify his mother when he checked into the hospital for the final time. She saw Ernie a few weeks before his death, while he was in the hospital for a periodic treatment. As was his habit, he never mentioned his illness. His mother recalled, "He talked about everybody else but himself. He wanted to know how everybody back home was doing. He never talked about himself."

Ernie did call Tony DeFilippo from the hospital. The lawyer deduced it was the end and that Ernie realized it. "He just asked how things were going," the lawyer related. "He said hello, but he never said good-bye."

Dr. Austin Weisberger, Ernie's personal physician, said, "There was a rapid acceleration of leukemia cells in the last few days, but before that Ernie functioned in a completely normal manner. He did everything without pain until he entered the hospital for the last time Thursday afternoon." At the hospital, Ernie was given heavy doses of medication in an attempt to shrink the malignant tissues and arrest the deterioration of his blood. He was also sedated with morphine. The treatment was unsuccessful.

Ernie's roommate, John Brown, was with a friend and his wife in a bar in Columbus, Ohio the night Ernie died. The friends had heard the news but kept it from Brown. "Precisely the time Ernie died, my eyes started smarting," recalled Brown. "At that time I didn't know he had died. We went to my friends apartment, and I later realized nobody turned on a radio there or in the car. Everybody started acting strange. Then I just started talking about Ernie for no reason. I know that sounds strange but it's true. The next day, when I was driving back to Cleveland, I heard the news on the radio."

Saturday, May 18, 1963, was a rainy day in Elmira, mirroring the mood of the city as news of Ernie's death spread. One of the first to hear the news was sportswriter Al Mallette. He recalled, "I heard about 4 a.m. Saturday. Although I knew it was coming, it was still a shock. It brought tears to my eyes. Everybody had lost. There's never been another like him."

The eulogies arrived from throughout the country. Ernie had touched people at every level and in every section of the nation. The themes were similar, Ernie Davis was a courageous gentleman and an inspiration to everyone.

Among those shocked by the news were members of Ernie's family. His aunt Angeline McLee of Uniontown, Pennsylvania told the Associated Press the family wasn't aware that Ernie was near death. "We didn't know at all," she said. "We were shocked. His mother didn't know but she thought I would have known. Ernie always confided in me. I was like a sister to him."

Art Modell said, "It will be a long time before we see a boy like Ernie Davis again. He was a great athlete, but more important, he was a great person. He is the finest boy I have ever met in my life." He announced that the Browns had retired Ernie's number 45, although he had only worn it in practice.

On hearing of Ernie's death, Syracuse University Chancellor William P. Tolley stated, "Ernie was as fine a man as he was an athlete—whether in the classroom, the dormitory or the playing field. He exemplified the highest standards of industry, integrity, responsibility and fidelity to duty."

Jim Brown said, "Ernie's death came as a complete shock to me. He was just the same right up until he went in the hospital." His physician, Dr. Weisberger said, "Ernie was a most impressive person. He was a real gentleman in all senses of the word. He had great courage and dignity. You couldn't help but admire him."

The three men who coached Ernie in football remembered him as more than a gifted athlete. His high school coach, Marty Harrigan, said, "Everyone knew Ernie's athletic greatness, but few realized what a great human he was. His concern for his fellow man, and his affection for children, was sincere." Ben Schwartzwalder of Syracuse University said, "Ernie was perfect. You hope you will find one like him and you never do. He was the friendliest, happiest kid I ever met. In spite of his great skill, he was humble, so much a team man that the other boys idolized him as their team leader." Blanton Collier, the new coach of the Cleveland Browns, said, "Ernie was one of the finest young men it was ever my privilege to coach. His death will be a great loss to all of us. Only those close to the situation realize what tremendous courage this young man displayed during this illness."

Ernie Davis' death was the lead story on both national press association wires, as thousands of words about him were sent into every newspaper, radio, and television newsroom in the country. Newspaper obituaries of famous people are sometimes written years in advance of their death. In November 1962, Al Mallette wrote Ernie's obituary for the Elmira *Star-Gazette*. He recalled, "It's the saddest thing I've ever done. I sweated and agonized over it. It's a difficult thing to do for a guy you loved."

Editorials and feature columns praising Ernie appeared in newspapers throughout the nation. Such respected sportswriters as Arthur Daley of *The New York Times* and Red Smith of the *New York Herald Tribune*, devoted articles to him. People everywhere were shocked and saddened. Many of the articles contained human interest stories of how Ernie had helped others. Charles Dotson, who worked at a pharmacy near the Syracuse University campus, told how he met Ernie during his senior year. They became friends, and when Ernie learned of Dotson's desire to enroll at Syracuse, he tried to assist him.

Former Syracuse freshman football coach Les Dye recalled an automobile ride from Elmira to Syracuse with Ernie and Tony DeFilippo. They saw a brush fire in a field and Ernie demanded that they stop the car. Dye recalled, "Ernie went into a nearby farm house and called the fire department. We had to wait until they arrived. 'Somebody might have been hurt,' Ernie said."

Ernie's mother requested that in lieu of flowers, donations should be sent to leukemia research. The Cleveland Browns and many others heeded her suggestion. Art Modell announced that the team had made a substantial contribution to start the Ernie Davis Foundation for Leukemia Research.

One letter accompanying a contribution was particularly poignant. Jim Brown recorded it, "Dr. Weisberger told me he recently received a letter from a little boy which touched him deeply. It read, 'I met Ernie Davis. He was so nice. I loved him. Here is 25 cents in his name to fight leukemia. I'll never forget him.'"

Ernie was eulogized in both houses of the United States Congress. In the Senate, Kenneth R. Keating (Rep. N.Y.) spoke in praise of Ernie and of the need to find a cure for cancer. The Senator stated, "Ernie Davis will be remembered not only for his prowess on the football field, but for the warm qualities and sincere humility which made him a fine human being." Keating supported the efforts of the Cleveland Browns and Ernie's mother in asking for contributions for leukemia research. He himself pledged a donation. Senator Jacob R. Javits (Rep. N.Y.) said, "I join in what he (Keating) has said and hope others will join in the cause which he has espoused with respect to the fight against cancer. I, myself, am sending a contribution as Ernie's mother has requested."

In the House of Representatives, Congressman R. Walter Riehlman (Rep. N.Y.) remarked, "It seems unfair that a young man of such great ability should be taken so young, but he left a monument to his memory: the good clean sportsmanship he practiced and the achievements he accomplished despite obstacles. All young people struggling along in life can look to his example for inspiration."

Few events have evoked a more heartfelt response from the citizens of Elmira than Ernie's funeral. As someone crassly but accurately observed, "It was the biggest thing to hit Elmira since Mark Twain." The Elmira Express had made his last stop. Those who attended the emotional event still recall it vividly. The cliche about there not being a dry eye at the services was, for once, appropriate.

The citizens of Elmira showed their feelings as 10,000 filed past the bier at the Neighborhood House where Ernie lay in state on Tuesday, May 21. The mourners came from all walks of life, dressed in work clothes and expensive dresses. At times, the line stretched for blocks and contained 200 persons. Most seemed shocked and disbelieving. A farmer, just in from his chores, was in the line. Asked if he knew Ernie a long time he responded, "No, I only met him once. He was delivering the mail and he stopped to talk with my family. He never mentioned who he was but we never forgot him."

Ernie's lying in state took place in the same gymnasium where he gained his early athletic success and spent hours honing his skills. His membership card, dated November 18, 1952, still remained in the files. Ernie had played in the gym less than a month before and always visited when he was in town. "He came two weeks ago too—but not to play," recalled Charles J. Kromer, executive director of Neighbohood House. "I asked him how he felt. He said, 'No different. I feel fine.' "

Due to previous commitments, the NFL spring meeting, Art Modell was unable to attend Wednesday's funeral. He did fly to Elmira on Tuesday to pay his respects to Ernie's mother. He also chartered a plane from Cleveland to fly players, office personnel, and media to the funeral. Included in the group were head coach Blanton Collier, Jim Brown, Lou Groza, Dick Schafrath, and John Wooten. Bobby Mitchell, for whom Ernie was traded to the Browns, was also on the plane. He recalled, "The times I met Ernie when I went back to Cleveland, I liked him. After all he didn't trade me. I was going to attend the funeral on my own when the Browns offered me a seat on their chartered plane. The funeral was very emotional. I've reflected on it over the years. It really impressed me the way all those people turned out like that."

All the schools in Elmira, both public and parochial, sent representatives, as did city, county, and state governments. All flags in the city were flown at half-mast. The mayor, Edward T. Lagonegro said, ". . .he gave this country an untarnished standard to guide its youth. . ."

The funeral was originally scheduled for the Monumental Baptist Church which Ernie attended, but organizers quickly realized that the church's small seating capacity would not accommodate all who wanted to attend. The service was switched to the larger First Baptist Church of Elmira, which also proved to be too small. Prior to the funeral service, Ernie's body lay in state at the church for three hours where thousands more viewed the bier. More than 1,600 persons jammed the church including the basement, while a crowd of 3,000 was in the park outside listening on speakers. The church was half-filled 75 minutes before the service was scheduled. The ceremony was conducted by five ministers including the Reverend Latta R. Thomas, pastor of Monumental Baptist Church.

Reverend Thomas quoted eight verses from first Corinthians, Chapter 15, emphasizing the passage, "But by the grace of God I am what I am. . .and His grace which was bestowed upon me was not in vain: but I labored more abundantly than they all: yet not I, but the grace of God which was with me."

He eulogized Ernie for living a life "like a free flowing stream which has both a living source and a free outlet. . .a life which reached outward to a sovereign God and fellow man." He said later, "The world stands in questioning awe when it sees the wedding of greatness and humility in the human spirit without realizing it is the humility which made the greatness genuine and beautiful." The Reverend W.C. Walser described Ernie as "Mr. Inspiration" to children.

The pallbearers, all former high school teammates, carried the coffin to the hearse for the mile and a half drive to the Woodlawn Cemetary, also the burial place of Mark Twain. Police estimated a 400-car procession escorted by 50 police vehicles made the trip. Those in the procession recalled that business activity ceased and people came out of their houses to watch in silence. Ernie was the first person buried in the Evergreen East section of the cemetary. When the funeral procession arrived, a small crowd had already gathered at the site. Those pepople had to park their cars outside the grounds and walk in because the cemetary gates were locked awaiting the hearse. The sun went behind the clouds as the procession stopped at the gravesite. The Reverend Thomas spoke briefly of Ernie's life and God, as many in the crowd of 1,500 sobbed. Someone cried, "I don't want to go on without him!" As the ceremony ended, the sun reappeared.

Police began to move the crowd out. Some observers plucked flower petals as mementos. Others left flowers. "Please, could I put these on the grave?"a boy inquired of a policeman who nodded. The boy knelt and placed the flowers. He turned and walked away. Children, families, and elderly couples paused at the grave before moving away. For hours afterward, people drove by in cars to pay their respects. One little boy walking with his mother said, "I bet he's the best person buried in this cemetary."

Ger Schwedes, the captain of Syracuse's 1959 National

Champions, summed up the feelings of many when he said, "Ernie was one of the finest football players, but more important, the finest gentlemen I've known. He had exceptional talent, but he was so humble. He never complained, always did what he was supposed to do, always went to class, and always strived for improvement in every phase of his life. He made all of us better athletes, better men. I'm just happy I was fortunate to have known him . . ."

Epilogue

Why? That question occurs to many, whenever a young person dies. When the person has extraordinary skill of unlimited potential, the question is more anguished. Despite knowing there was no cure for leukemia, many were convinced Ernie had overcome the disease. Maybe because we wanted him to. It disrupts our sense of security when a young athlete like Ernie dies. We all become more vulnerable. If it could happen to Ernie Davis, it could happen to me.

Ernie's death had a lasting impact on everyone who knew him, but particularly his peers. When a friend with a tremendous future dies it stuns you. For most it was their first encounter with dying. It was a part of the future they had never previously considered. For the first time they contemplated death as well as life. Maybe they too didn't have as much time as they anticipated. You try to reconcile why an Ernie Davis dies. You never really can.

For some, at least, the most difficult aspect of Ernie Davis' life was his quiet acceptance of his death. Why was he able to face it so equably? The difficulty may be because he didn't act the way he was expected. There were no complaints, no binges, no regrets. There was uncommon dignity. It was as extraordinary a performance as any he had on the athletic field.

He knew he was dying. He knew that he had tried his best against leukemia. He knew he had accomplished a great deal during his short life. The only thing left was to say good-bye. In his last weeks he visited the people and places he loved. He made his farewells as cheerful as possible to spare his friends. He provided them with a lasting memory. That's why they remember him more as a man than an athlete. As a person he lives on in the memories of those who know him and were touched by him. In 1979 he was elected to the National Football Foundation College Hall of Fame. Many felt the honor was long overdue. He was the third player from Syracuse and second from Elmira to be so honored. As an athlete, winner of the Heisman Trophy and a member of the Hall of Fame, he will be remembered as long as football is played.

In Elmira and Syracuse, the normal changes time makes on all our lives have occurred. There have been personal changes—Ernie's mother has divorced and remarried; Chuck Davis is contemplating retiring from the New York City goverement; Marty Harrigan no longer coaches football, and recently retired as Elmira Free Academy high school principal; former high school basketball coach Jim Flynn is retired; Tony DeFilippo still is a law partner with his brother, but spends part of the winter in Florida; Ben Schwartzwalder retired in 1973 after 25 years as head football coach at Syracuse with a record of 153-91-3 and was recently elected into the College Football Hall of Fame.

Ernie's peers are now well established in their career fields. Bill Fitzgerald in education, Jack Moore in law, John Brown in banking, and John Mackey in oil, banking and real estate. It would be expected that these relations and friends would have fond memories of Ernie, but the depth of their feeling and the persistance of their loyalty is an awesome tribute. There have been physical changes also. Ernie's house in Elmira has been torn down and the Ernie Davis Park is now on the site. At the time of Ernie's death, a new Elmira Free Academy was being built on Hoffman Street. The building where Ernie attended EFA was to become a junior high school when construction of the new high school was completed. Two EFA students, Jack Lundy and Nan Linderberry collected over 3,000 signatures on a petition to name the new school in memory of Ernie Davis.

The school board, with the assistance of Tony De-Filippo, passed the following resolution: ". . .be it resolved that when the present Elmira Free Academy building on Lake Street becomes a junior high school in 1964, it will be designated in honor and memory of Ernie Davis."

Dr. Jack E. Thomas, then school board president, explained the decision. "It is particularly appropriate that the school building Ernie attended bear his name while the name he so honored, Elmira Free Academy, with all its tradition, be preserved by designating the new senior high school Elmira Free Academy." Previously, the school board had voted to name the junior high school Samuel Clemens (Mark Twain).

There have been numerous changes to the Syracuse University campus. The one Ernie would immediately recognize is that Archbold Stadium has been razed, and the Carrier Dome erected on the site. When it was being built, the Syracuse students, some of whom were not even born when Ernie last played for Syracuse, began a campaign to have the stadium named in his honor. Their attempt was unsuccessful, but their efforts did result in the establishment of an Ernie Davis Memorial Room. Moreover, the students have kept up the pressure for maintaining the integrity of the memorial, persuading the university to set aside an appropriate area for Ernie's memorabilia in the room which is used for social gatherings.

The quality of Ernie's life is exemplified by the powerful impact his presence still has on family and friends so many years later. Many of these men and women are sophisticated people, who have experienced life and its many aspects, yet a kleenex was as important as a tape recorder at interviews.

However, the scenes were not maudlin. Everyone spoke of Ernie's life positively. The common themes were that it had been a privilege to know Ernie Davis and that because of his example their lives had been improved. His courage gave them courage. We aren't all professional athletes, but we are all going to die. We can all attempt to emulate the courage, humility and grace Ernie demonstrated during his illness.

The question most often raised about Ernie Davis' athletic ability is whether he would have surpassed Jim Brown in the pros as he had in college. Obviously that question can't be answered. Football potential is impossible to judge accurately, which is why some college stars never make it in the pros, while college unknowns can become pro stars. Until they can measure what's inside a player that will always be the rule. It can be said unequivocally that inside Ernie Davis beat the heart of a champion. Ben Schwartzwalder said, "When you talk about Ernie Davis, you're treading on hallowed ground. We always thought he had a halo around him and now we know he has."